THE CHURCH
AND
CHRISTIAN BELIEF

The Church
and
Christian Belief

by

Otto Semmelroth

Translated by

Thomas R. Milligan

(With Study-Club Questions)

DEUS BOOKS
PAULIST PRESS
(Paulist Fathers)
Glen Rock, New Jersey

A Deus Books Edition of the Paulist Press, 1966, by special arrangement with Verlag Butzon and Bercker Kevelaer.

NIHIL OBSTAT:
Rev. James J. O'Connor
    Censor Librorum

IMPRIMATUR:
✠ Leo A. Pursley, D.D.
Bishop of Fort Wayne — South Bend
July 22, 1966

The Nihil Obstat and Imprimatur are official declarations that a book or pamphlet is free of doctrinal or moral error. No implication is contained therein that those who have granted the Nihil Obstat and Imprimatur agree with the contents, opinions or statements expressed.

Library of Congress
Catalog Card Number: 66-26962

Cover Design: Claude Ponsot

Published by the Paulist Press
Editorial Office: 304 W. 58th St., N. Y., N. Y. 10019
Business Office: Glen Rock, New Jersey 07452

Printed and bound in the United States
of America by Our Sunday Visitor Press

Contents

I
THE WORD OF GOD
Biblical Inspiration:
Nature and Significance for Salvation

II
WHAT IS FAITH?
Nature and Shape of Christian Belief

5

III
WHY THE CHURCH?
What the Catholic Church Claims and What She Is

IV
NO SALVATION OUTSIDE THE CHURCH?
The Members of Christ's Body

V
CRITICISM OF THE CHURCH
A Right and Its Limits

I
The Word of God

Biblical Inspiration:
Nature and Significance for Salvation

INTRODUCTION

L IKE all matters of Christian faith, the Christian doctrine of the divine inspiration of Sacred Scripture
can be viewed in a variety of different ways. Naturally
we shall disregard that "point of view" (and it no
longer is really a point of view) which has lost insight
into the Word of God because of human indifference or
sinful remoteness from God. However, even where
Christian faith is still taken seriously, the Bible seems
to evoke a wide variety of responses. It might be approached without any commitment whatsoever. It might
also be approached with an attitude of genuine involvement — an involvement which could remain on the
purely human level of serious confrontation or which
might involve the bond of real faith.

From *the viewpoint of the history of religion,* the
Bible is seriously regarded as a document containing
the origins of the Christian faith, but this viewpoint
does not see the call for personal decision in the Bible.
The biblical message puts no questions to man, no

challenge involving the basic pattern of his living. The Bible is evaluated in the same way as are the written documents of other religions, such as the Koran of Mohammedanism, the Talmud of post-Christian Judaism or the sacred, Oriental writings of Buddhism. Because religion is a worthy object of research as one of the phenomena of the history of human ideas, it is important to investigate the Bible *objectively* and impartially. From this viewpoint one must not be personally affected by the contents of these writings; it is in fact detrimental, because it is subjective.

A second point of view is one in which the student of the Bible is indeed prepared to be impressed by scriptural pronouncements and even to become obligated by these. This point of view, however, somehow remains *extrinsic*. The criterion as to whether and to what extent one makes a commitment is, in this approach, not the biblical statements in and of themselves. The norm is rather the *insight of one's own understanding* that finds itself stimulated by the scriptural word. There is no need for suspicion whenever reading and meditation on the biblical text make a deep impression and affect the will and feelings. On the contrary, it is precisely this personal effect of the observed text that one is seeking. There is, however, still no question here of real faith. For this view is no different from the way in which one experiences Goethe or reads the sacred books of Buddhism. The search here is for documents of wisdom, such as are found in all religions, and so the Christian Bible is also welcomed as a source of such wisdom. Yet the approach remains a very *literary* one. This kind of involvement ultimately lacks commitment and thus remains quite remote from the Christian way of being effectively influenced by the inspired Bible. The value of this viewpoint lies in its positive attitude, the open-mindedness with which the reader lets himself be taught. The questionable element is the danger of being all too ready to accept whatever presents itself under the guise of wisdom, even if it is nonsense. From the Christian standpoint we must reject this position because it is not enough simply to value the Bible positively, if we are unwilling to regard it as a divine book set apart from all other writings.

And so we come to the third point of view: belief in the Bible as a document of faith *inspired by God*. What drives the Christian toward Sacred Scripture and causes him to venerate it is a call to commitment, which lives within this book not by reason of the wisdom and authority of the human author but rather because of a *direct influence of God,* which we call *inspiration* and which remains present throughout all of the historical evolution and human writing of these books. Whoever opens Sacred Scripture and reads with such a faith, enters into a sacred realm that separates him from the profane and determines his whole outlook — something that always happens whenever man is confronted with God's holiness and realizes his own sinfulness. We find this in the prophet Isaiah, when he was called by God (Is. 6, 1-13); in Peter, after the marvelous catch of fish: "Depart from me, for I am a sinful man, O Lord" (Luke 5, 8). We find it in Thomas, confronted with the risen Christ: "My Lord and my God!" (John 20, 28).

We encounter difficulties precisely because of this uniquely right attitude toward Sacred Scripture. We confront Sacred Scripture prepared to take it seriously, to weigh its words, so to speak, on the meditative scales of our spirit. We cannot regard the Bible simply as a book of stories having no obligation for us, a book concerning which it does not matter what we believe.

Because of our faith in the divinely inspired Bible, we are put under obligation by that Bible. However, obligation can only come to us from truth, not from legend and myth.

Yet, even the believer cannot overlook the fact that the Bible cannot and will not be taken as literally in all of its texts as we take official documents: word for word, just as they are written. The literal sense of the words of many biblical utterances contradicts our experience and knowledge too much for us to be able to interpret them just as they are written. That the rabbit is not a cud-chewing animal is so undeniable that the contrary statement in the Bible cannot be regarded as objective truth — just to indicate one example among many others. We too readily expect from the scriptural revelation of God the same documentary style we find in our law books or in the explicit language of our textbooks. Yet, the question remains whether this criterion is correct. After all, we are not surprised in other situations when people of extraordinary intelligence express their wisdom and knowledge in a way that sounds like a foreign language to the man in the street.

We must ask ourselves in what sense we are to understand Sacred Scripture. God has of course breathed his Word into the Bible so that we can draw it forth by reading and meditation. Certainly we do this under the guidance of the Holy Spirit, but we are also dependent on the word as written and as we understand it. Therefore it is a very urgent task to see Sacred Scripture in the proper light.

In order to understand properly the nature of inspiration, it is necessary first to clarify the problem about the meaning and purpose of this reality. In the concern over the question of *what,* the question of the *why* and *wherefore* of faith is often very much ne-

glected. Many will be alarmed at this and say, defensively, that at a time when too much emphasis is being
placed on the purpose and the utility of everything, we
should not also pay homage to this utilitarianism in
matters of faith. Nevertheless, the question of meaning
and purpose is an urgent one, for faith and theology
are concerned with the truths of *salvation.* Salvation
however is essentially history, dealing with the events
and actions of God. What else is this saving and
sanctifying action of God in history but the drive toward
a goal, the dynamic purpose or *wherefore,* the direction
toward an end which carries over into the beyond? In
matters of salvation, and thus of biblical inspiration,
knowledge of the *wherefore* answers the question of
the *what.*

THE MEANING AND PURPOSE
OF BIBLICAL INSPIRATION

Different Approaches

I would like to make a rather random observation
about the history of dogma. The teaching of the
Church's magisterium on the inspiration of Sacred
Scripture shows noteworthy differences. We could, in
fact, distinguish here two different kinds of pronouncements. The distinguishing feature is the way in which a
particular pronouncement characterizes the working of
the inspiration of God. The mode of expression is different. Naturally the two classifications do not exclude
one another. What one doctrinal definition sets forth
cannot be denied by a different one, but different approaches nevertheless are evident here.

To the *first classification* belong the solemn doctrinal definitions of the Council of Trent (1546) and of Vatican Council I (1870). These two councils are separated by almost three and a half centuries. However, they are closer to one another in the question we are considering than are pronouncements of the *second type,* separated from the time of Vatican Council I by only a few decades. This second category covers the encyclicals of the recent popes on Scripture: *Providentissimus Deus* of Leo XIII (1893), *Spiritus paraclitus* of Benedict XV (1920), and *Divino afflante Spiritu* of Pius XII (1943). We can also add the condemnation of Modernist errors concerning Sacred Scripture under Pius X in 1907.

Then, what are the different *viewpoints* — not the contradictions — that distinguish the two categories? The more recent documents very strongly stress *inerrancy* as the operative element in the authorship of the divinely inspired Scriptures. Thus an *objective and impersonal* point of view is dominant here. On the other hand, in the documents of Trent and Vatican I, primary emphasis is given to the statement: "God is the *author* of Sacred Scripture," as the operative element in inspiration. In this approach the *personal* emphasis predominates, while the epistemological and impersonal emphasis on biblical inerrancy is not expressly mentioned at all. In fact, the significance of inerrancy seems to be minimized when Vatican I says that the biblical books are canonical, i.e., were included by the Church in the canon of biblical books, "not merely because they contain divine revelation without error, but because [these books], written at the prompting of the Holy Spirit, have God as their author, and as such have been given over to the care of the Church" (Denz. 1787).

Neither view should be played off against the other.

In all the documents mentioned, the one approach always implies the other. Whenever God's authorship is emphasized in the biblical books, their inerrancy is also implicitly taught. Whenever inerrancy of the inspired Bible is affirmed, it is on the basis that these books have God as their author. However, the fact that, in the more recent documents, the impersonal and epistemological aspect is so strongly emphasized does show that this particular approach in the teaching of the Church reflects the general intellectual climate of our times, when the accent has shifted from the personal to the impersonal (against which the personalism of our day is so desperately rebelling). In our approach to the Bible we must take care not to carry over this one-sided tendency toward depersonalization, which characterizes the mentality of our era, without supplementing it with a personal view. The insistence of the later documents that Sacred Scripture is without error must always be understood in the light of the personal view of inspiration enunciated by Trent and Vatican I. Accordingly, in the later documents, we should not overlook the personal factor; we should also make it an interpretive principle there as well as in the earlier ones. This will preserve us from an anticipation that would necessarily be bitterly disappointed by the actual ambiguity and uncertainty of the biblical text. From the ancient Catholic realization that Sacred Scripture simply cannot be its own interpreter, we must draw the conclusion that the Bible cannot be the same kind of source of objective knowledge as is straight factual information or the knowledge we get from the teaching of the Church. Anyone who would seek to understand scriptural inerrancy solely, or even primarily, as meaning the communication of factual knowledge is doomed to an insoluble and painful vacillation in his thinking.

In reality, the fact that truth without error is offered us in Sacred Scripture must be considered in the light of personal understanding that in Sacred Scripture we are encountering God, whose Word is never without its works and who, therefore, along with the inspiration of the biblical Word has promised his works of grace to the person who seeks after this Word. Conversely, however, this personal sense of the Scriptures, as the announcement that God himself is communicating with us, must be also understood as meaning that the content of what God says to us is true. For a person can never communicate without revealing something of himself. This will be made clear in what follows.

Two Aspects of Truth

There are two kinds of knowledge. I do not mean here the difference between faith and knowledge strictly so-called — the difference being that faith perceives truth on the *witness* of another person, whereas in knowledge truth is perceived by reason of *one's own personal apprehension*. I am not concerned with the difference in the way in which truth is perceived. I am concerned with a difference involving the *meaning and purpose* that guide our perception of truth.

One mode of perceiving truth involves an objective and impersonal grasp of reality. Whether truth is grasped through one's own insight and investigation or whether it is communicated to us by a teacher, does not matter as long as the object of truth is, so to speak, cognitively absorbed. Thus, to fulfill God's mandate to him to subject the world to himself, man must know and explore the nature of this world. Such natural knowledge today results only rarely in a genuine awe, untrammeled by practical considerations, in the presence of a mysterious world; it does not result in the praise of the God who created such a world. Man is much more interested in opening up the possibilities that the world offers for human plans and achievements. Natural knowledge is seen as the instrument by which the world is made more adaptable to technological development. Such knowledge therefore serves for mastery and utilization of the world — something by no means unjustified, since man as the image of God is supposed to be the master of this world. The Protestant theologian, Paul Tillich, has very aptly called such knowledge "knowledge for the sake of control".

This kind of knowledge and perception of truth is characterized by two features. It is first concerned with the results or the content of what we know in order to make it accessible to practical human use. This kind of knowledge must be available to anyone who seeks it and, furthermore, must be as precise as possible, unambiguous (at least for those comprehending it), statable and so impersonal that it is divorced as completely as possible from the limitations of human subjectivity. Secondly, it is not actually important *who* facilitates the grasp of such truth. Whether this or that teacher communicates it, or whether it is learned without a teacher, is not important. The person is not the important factor here but, rather, the thing about which he is speaking. The person is ancillary to the objective content, to the thing whose knowledge and mastery he is to be an instrument in procuring.

There is, however, another kind of perception of truth by the human mind. As in the case of the mode of perception discussed above, here too the mind functions as a human organ tending toward truth. Here too objective reality becomes known truth, but the perception of the communicated content now involves the encounter with the *person* who has communicated it. The effort is now made to understand the perceptible content of knowledge, not for its own sake but for the sake of the person who in communicating this content has revealed something of himself. Even insignificant details now loom large, because in them is illuminated the countenance of the person who in his utterance has expressed his own presence and thus something about himself. Even when someone makes an inconsequential remark about the weather, in order to overcome the awkwardness of a first meeting, such a remark does not really mean: "The weather is fine today," but rather: "I consider this fine weather." The statement is rich, not because of its objective content but because it testifies to the deeds and desires of the person who has his experience, feels it and describes it to another person in order that he will share in it.

There is no question here of knowledge for the sake of control. The person who is communicating is certainly communicating himself, but he must not on that account be received to be mastered and utilized as if he were an object. This kind of knowledge also manifests the person who is communicating. Of course the content of what is said cannot be disregarded. How could one really heed the person talking if one disregarded *what* the person is saying? In receiving the content of the utterance, one says "Yes" to the person who is speaking through that utterance. In impersonal knowledge (knowledge for the sake of control), the communicating person is subordinate to the subject to be learned. Here, on the other hand, knowledge of the subject is subordinate to *personal confrontation*. In listening, one perceives the person and does so with a readiness to communicate himself in answering.

Sacred Scripture as the Voice of God's Personal Word

Whoever gives undue emphasis to inerrancy as an effect of biblical inspiration, is not far removed from the temptation of expecting from Sacred Scripture a kind of knowledge for the sake of control. He runs the risk of making God's authorship serve a knowledge that is unequivocal, without error, free of doubt, and capable of being placed in neat impersonal pigeonholes. Instead, it ought to be especially emphasized that the Bible has God as its author. Thus the content of the inerrant Scriptures should be put in the service of a personal encounter with the living God, who wants to be met in meditation on the Bible and who wants to communicate himself in grace. The meaning and purpose of biblical knowledge are not a knowledge for the sake of control to be used to practical advantage or ethically applied. The effort expended in understanding the content of biblical statements should be regarded as a fulfillment of the encounter with God. In the inspired, that is to say Spirit-filled, scriptural book, he wished to give a pledge that the spirit of his grace would be effectual wherever this book was faithfully read and lovingly meditated on. It is therefore also important, of course, *what* one reads in the Bible. It is still more important, however, *that* one read it and meditate upon it in order to open the doors of one's own spirit to the Spirit of God. Therefore, the effort to understand the Bible's content becomes truly meaningful when it results not merely in understanding but also when it becomes a genuine response in the prayerful self-revelation of man toward God.

Consequently, it is no longer so terribly surprising that the Church's scholarship has not been able to explain everything up till now. In fact, much that was thought to be clear is again becoming uncertain. Pius XII writes in his encyclical, *Divino afflante Spiritu:* "If the desired solution is long in coming and a successful outcome is not granted us, but may be reserved only for later generations, then no one can really complain about that . . . Nor would it be too surprising if a completely satisfying answer might never be found for one or another of the questions that plague us" (*A.A.S.* 35, 1943, p. 318). When one seeks to interpret the scriptural Word in order to encounter the person of God revealing himself there, the encounter with him in such interpretative efforts is fulfilled even if the content of the text cannot be expressed in unequivocal assertions. Even among human beings we know that the effort to understand a letter from a friend in terms of its deeper meanings, which we know are intended but still not perfectly obvious, often brings before the reader the person of the sender, with all his familiar habits and characteristic surroundings.

In this connection it may be worth noting that even the writing style of our theological textbooks — although they treat their material in typical textbook fashion almost too impersonally — does not completely conceal the personal character of this material. At least in the Latin textbooks the titles of the individual treatises express this character to a certain degree. What we find designated in German theological textbooks as "Divine Doctrine", the "Doctrine of the Incarnation and Redemption", the "Doctrine of Grace", the "Sacraments" and the "Last Things", is titled much more personally in the Latin terminology: *De Deo Uno et Trino* (On the One and Triune God), *De Deo Creante* (God the Creator), *De Deo Redemptore* (God the Redeemer), *De Deo Sanctificante* (God the Sanctifier — i.e., the doctrine of grace), *De Deo Consummatore*

(God the Fulfiller). What these titles clearly suggest applies in a much more immediate way to Sacred Scripture, which with good reason is called the Word of God. It is the voice of personal encounter with God within the context of the Church.

SPECIAL QUESTIONS ABOUT INSPIRATION

In the light of this definition of inspiration, we may now examine three points that clarify, to some extent, the nature of inspiration itself. These are: first, the question of inerrancy as a consequence of divine inspiration; second, the question of *occurrence;* third, the question of the *scope* of scriptural inspiration.

The Inerrancy of the Bible

We must try to uderstand scriptural inerrancy from the standpoint of the personal meaning of the inspired Bible. If we approach the matter from a purely impersonal and objective point of view, as is so often done in the popular manuals of today, then we would have to consider as dishonest or false the statement by the Church that the Bible is in all things true and without error.

The biblical authors wanted of course to write a narrative of events and represent the world in which they lived. However, they were not primarily concerned with objective historicity and impersonal description of their world; rather, they were concerned with history and the world as dating and locating a process of salvation in which a personal God asserts himself and makes his claims known to men. In order to set forth this divine and personal dimension in the context of the world and in the events of history, the authors let shine forth the personal countenance of God, who participates and gives of himself within history and within the structure of the world. This happens to such an extent in their writing that the world and history lose most of their objectivity.

The God of salvation did not proclaim himself to man through his works only during those times and in those events reported in the Bible; rather, this same God intends to graciously communicate himself also to everyone who reads the biblical account of God's involvement in those earlier times. This personal mystery of God and his work of salvation is etched in such vivid relief in Scripture that the pure historicity of the events, their sequence, interconnection, perspective, and even their particular concrete shape, are largely glossed over or go unmentioned.

The Bible describes history in order that we may encounter the God of salvation. That is why the Bible presents with such urgency the countenance of the personal God in the course of historical events. That is why it clothes its teachings concerning the personal God in the garments of heroic narrative and didactic poetry. That is why, in the letters of apostolic admonition, it views the historical situation of the various communities in the light of divine judgment for the sake of all generations. Thus the Bible describes history almost in the same way that modern artists portray people: so that a deeply hidden personal mystery can be depicted precisely as the artist understands it; the natural human features get distorted — or so it seems to the non-artist. And yet the artist would consider it unforgivable if anyone were to tell him that the picture did not represent the person it was supposed to repre-

sent. The person is represented all right, but in the
sense that the artist has caught the mystery and uniqueness of that person's spirit. That is the way biblical
imagery works in representing the mystery of the person of God, who acts in the world through history
shaping it for mankind so that it may become the
history of salvation. In these historical events God has
acted for and upon mankind. In the account of these
events God wants to call every person, everyone who
reads this account of God's turning to mankind, this
account of the decision made by the people of those
times for or against him.

The teaching of the Church emphasizes very strongly
that, if we wish to interpret the biblical Word, we must
first be well aware of the *literary* form in which a particular book of the Bible is written. This means in
different books there will be different ways in which
statements are meant to be understood. In principle
this means that we must approach the Bible with a
readiness to take its statements in terms of the unique
meaning of Scripture. In contrast, our approach in
reading and interpreting modern texts cannot be the
criterion. The same principles that guided biblical
authors in framing and arranging their utterances must
also guide the search for the correct meaning of the
biblical text. "Biblical authors" sometimes means entire
generations of people of the Old Testament, or the
historical tradition of the New Testament within which
God's inspiration is at work. Anyone who tries to
interpret biblical sayings and metaphors according to
the criteria of modern objective historical writing, and
then proceeds to demonstrate that things simply could
not have been that way at all, does not convict the
Bible of error but, rather, convicts himself of deficient
understanding. The Bible is true and without error,

but only in the way indicated by its meaning and purpose: seeing history and the world as giving utterance to the God who personally manifests himself and brings about a supernatural salvation. Such utterance cannot, however, be understood merely from narrow analysis of the written word nor from a superficial reading.

Even to get the dimmest notion of what the truth of the biblical message is requires a careful search into the depths of scriptural metaphors, enlivened by one's own experience of God. The person approaching Scripture superficially and from the outside is content with demonstrating that biblical statements differ substantially from other evidence concerning the same events, or differ from what human science has been able to determine with certainty. The person of faith, on the other hand, realizing the workings of God's grace, will see in what proper and deeper sense the biblical message is true.

The Occurrence of Biblical Inspiration

Our second question concerns the occurrence of biblical inspiration. The right answer to this can be found only if the question itself is changed a little. The question should not be concerned with the occurrence of inspiration as a *process;* instead, it should be concerned with the inspired book as the palpable *result* of a process that remains shrouded in mystery in its beginnings and actual individual occurrences. It may well be helpful to find out how God brings forth a book which may be called his, without that book ceasing to be the work of human authors. More important however is the product, the result, the inspired book itself, in which the Church and her individual members have available an organ in which the invisible God, no longer physically present, has been manifested.

In the same way, Christianity at first engaged in much controversy concerning the correct understanding of the incarnation and how it came about. However, these disputes were important because of the outcome, i.e., that here is a human being, in looking at whom we see God, in whom therefore we can meet God, just as we meet another human being, but with the certainty that through this intimate divine encounter we are sharers in the triune God. In the case of Scripture, also, we naturally wanted to know how God could have inspired it in such a way that it resulted in his authorship of this document. One wonders where the inspiration may have begun to take its effect. This amounts to asking which individual persons God granted his inspiration to, or, more pointedly, what capacities and powers of these individuals does the inspiration of God permeate, so that God can be the author of the resultant book. It should not be overlooked that this (not unjustified) pointing of the question involves certain dangers.

For example, we seem to be blind to the possibility that perhaps it was not merely a matter of one individual person, struck at his writing desk by the inspiration of God. By a special external and internal providence, divine inspiration may well have been able to *penetrate history,* ensuring the book's composition and its later possession by the Church as her divinely guaranteed text. Research in the history of the formation and editing of the biblical books has now undeniably shown that not only the Old Testament but also the New Testament writings need not have been the private property of one author. They could have been

edited on the basis of traditions stemming from various
and long existing sources. We thus seem to be presented
with the following alternatives: (1) God's inspiration
starts in the mind and will of an individual person,
who gave the book its final form as we know it — in
which case God would make his inspirational authorship effective in a work that was only partly editorial
in nature; (2) Inspiration means that the present book
is an essential part of the Church and so, like the
Church herself, is the result of God's guidance throughout a long history of salvation — in which case it would
of course remain true that inspiration permeates human
activity, illuminating the human mind, motivating the
human will and determining the course of human
action. However, which persons have been inspired by
the Spirit of God, and when and where, it is not at all
possible to determine absolutely. Nor is this necessary.
It may be regrettable, but it may also be a valuable sign,
that close study of the sources has up to now led only to
negative results, i.e., that the human authors of certain
books of the Bible were not the people to whom a
long tradition had attributed them, even though the
attribution was no doubt based on what seemed like
compelling reasons.

The salvific meaning of Sacred Scripture requires
only that we know what the Church's canon declares:
these writings are the product of a special divine guidance and supernatural agency which, by inspiration,
has assured the composition of this book and has entrusted it to the Church as the central organ of man's
divine life. As long as this happened, it is quite im-
material whether God's inspiration affected one person
or many, or even whether it was active throughout a
whole long series of centuries. Consequently, we need
not be surprised when, for example, an author's name

mentioned in the scriptural text turned out to be wrong in the present-day sense. If it was then the custom to practice pseudepigraphy (i.e., the attribution of a manuscript to someone not the author), then we might expect this to be the practice in the inspired Bible. In that case it would not be a lie, or a deception, but rather a custom not uncommon at the time. Of course whether that is actually the case in certain passages of the Bible would have to be determined by careful and circumspect scientific investigation.

We are the more receptive to all of this if we keep in mind that, in regard to occurrence of inspiration, it is far less a matter of our somehow "listening in" on the mysterious activity of the inspiring God, than of receiving the result: i.e., that here in one God himself is so very much the author, that in reading this book we are receiving the pledge of God's gracious promise and his gracious communication of himself to us.

Still another danger can arise through putting the accent in the wrong place when discussing the occurrence of inspiration. This is the danger of an impersonal objectification in the treatment of Sacred Scripture. Whoever investigates the process of inspiration only because he is concerned solely with absolute inerrancy and with the clear exposition of revealed truths would necessarily be plagued by the question of why God could not have expressed himself a little more clearly in his revelation. It would be incomprehensible to him why God did not arrange his truth systematically, as in a textbook on theology, and did not clearly codify his will for man, as in a law book. We should, however, look upon this book primarily as one in which God has revealed himself by inspiration, so that in meditating on it we may find him again as the God who throughout the long years of history prepared for the salvation of mankind and who wants to impart this salvation to us, even as we read. Then we need no longer be disturbed either by the often tortured analysis of God's inspirational process, or by the ambiguities that often make a mockery of our desire for clear-cut results. "God become Word" is also received whenever the Church, on her journey through the centuries, endeavors to grasp the divine sense of God's Word and whenever the individual perceives this sense with certainty, not from the text itself but rather from its interpretation by the Church.

The Scope of Inspiration

Finally, from the foregoing analysis we find that the question concerning the scope of inspiration will receive an answer both narrower and broader than the answer that is sometimes given.

Modern man is not the first to discover that faith in the inspiration of Sacred Scripture and in its guaranteed inerrancy faces all kinds of difficulties because of the absurdities, apparent contradictions, historical and factual impossibilities encountered in an actual reading of the Bible. Even the early Church Fathers found themselves compelled to discuss such matters, even though the individual points that they felt to be difficult were different from what they are now. Theological endeavors in modern times have often tried to do away with these difficulties through recourse to a milder application to the dogma of inspiration, through restricting the scope or the extent of inspiration. The attempt to exclude from inspiration scientific and historical matters, or the above-mentioned matters of detail found in the Bible, has run counter to the teaching authority

of the Church. Nor is anything gained by the attempt
to abandon the concept of *verbal inspiration* — the view
that God's inspiration gave the scriptural authors their
text word for word — in favor of a concept of *essential
inspiration* — the view that God inspired only the basic
content while leaving the formulations of this content
up to the human authors. The nature of inspiration
itself could very easily be distorted by such considerations.

If it is true that biblical inspiration, as an overall
divine guidance by means of external and internal influence on events and people, has brought about this book
as God's book for his Church, then this must also hold
true with regard to the book as it now exists. The entire
book, with all its parts and sentences and words, is the
inspired Word of God, the bearer of his inspiration. In
individual cases it may sometimes be doubtful whether
a particular text belongs to the original content of the
inspired book. It is also hardly possible to determine
whether divine inspiration extended to the sentences
and words or simply to the content expressed by them.
The guiding action of the inspiring God permeates
everything that belongs to this book as produced. Inspiration permeates Scripture as the soul permeates the
human body. Previously there has been a too one-sided
interest in inspiration in this or that individual writer,
instead of interest in the book as resulting from God's
influence — an influence always at work wherever anything contributed toward bringing this book about.
Thus it was possible to misunderstand inspiration as a
kind of dictation, like speaking into a tape recorder.
No doubt the attempt to distinguish between verbal and
essential inspiration is grounded in this very misunderstanding. In such a distinction inspiration is something
like an executive dictating to his secretary by giving her

only the content of what he wants to have written; this would illustrate essential inspiration. In another instance he might dictate word for word and require that the secretary record it all verbatim; this would illustrate verbal inspiration.

The flaw in this comparison is that the person dictating and the secretary are situated opposite one another. The inspiring God, on the other hand, does not stand opposite the biblical writer and the long history of development in Scripture. With his special providence he penetrates to the very heart of the long history of tradition; he penetrates the innermost being of the human persons who participate in bringing the books of the Bible into existence, making his presence effective in the mind and the will. He does not dictate words and sentences; instead, he is present when the human being plans and writes, just as he has permeated the course of history from which in its various elements the written word of the Bible has emerged. This Bible is filled with the activity of God, not only because it gives an account of God's action but also because it has resulted from his action and communicates this action to whoever reads and ponders Scripture. Therefore it is *not* a matter of indifference whether a person makes the scriptural text his own by immersing himself in the biblical narrative, or whether the contents of the Bible are handed to him on a silver platter through the skilled second-hand presentation of a human commentator.

THE INSPIRED BIBLE AND THE CHURCH'S MAGISTERIUM

Our discussion up to this point seems to push aside to a certain extent the problem of understanding Sacred

Scripture in terms of its verbal content, in terms of its
clearly statable truths. It may seem that the aim of
seeking a personal encounter with God is so much in
the foreground that the substance and content of the
Bible seem almost beside the point. This impression is
correct only insofar as conversion to God and personal
response to his saving power are primary goals. Knowledge of biblical content is, however, by no means excluded or even to be treated lightly. We know, for
example, that human beings cannot communicate with
one another without expressing themselves in statements that have meaningful content. The person of the
speaker is really grasped only when the listener seriously considers what he has to say. In the same way Sacred
Scripture, precisely as an instrument of mutual encounter between God and man, must be received and
interpreted on the level of its content.

Now we face a problem that is not quite solved by
the insights we have gathered up to now. This is the
question of how we can achieve clarity and certainty
as to what content is actually being communicated to
us in the individual books, chapters and verses of Sacred
Scripture. Here Scripture itself leaves us pretty much
in the dark. This is why we are bound by the Church's
pronouncements in our dealings with the Bible. There
is yet another reason. Since the Bible in the life of the
Church must become, instead of a dead book, a living
organ of encounter with God, it can be effective only
within the living reality of the Church. Since Scripture,
in the greater part of its content, cannot be its own
interpreter, the living Church is constituted as authentic
guardian and living interpreter of biblical content. Thus
our point of departure has led us straight to the question of the Bible's place in the teaching of the Church.
The situation can be stated in two ways: Sacred Scrip-

ture is the point of departure providing the content for the teaching of the Church; only within the teaching of the Church can we find Sacred Scripture.

Sacred Scripture as the Starting Point of the Church's Teaching

There can be no doubt that the teaching Church has the task of interpreting Sacred Scripture under the guidance of the Holy Spirit, whom Christ himself promised to the Church for this purpose. This is really only the counterpart to the assertion that the only entrance into Sacred Scripture is through the Church's proclamation. If the believing Christian is sent to the teaching Church for the interpretation of Sacred Scripture, then of course the Church has the task of meeting this need. It also follows that the teaching Church has the obligation of proclaiming God's revelation to mankind. However, Sacred Scripture is a visible form of this revelation as the apostles proclaimed it. Hence the Church is clearly constituted in a special way as the interpreting proclaimer of Scripture.

In this positive sense it is therefore undeniable that Scripture belongs to the content of the Church's teaching. Yet, there are also reasons for understanding this assertion in an exclusive sense, namely, that actually the Church has nothing other than Scripture to proclaim, interpret and expound to mankind. This of course would be correct only if the entire revelation of God as it is basically constituted is contained at least essentially in Sacred Scripture, so that from it this revelation can be brought forth through the actions of the Church under the guidance of the Holy Spirit. Naturally this view must be kept free of misconceptions represented in the 16th-century Reformation principle: *Sola Scriptura.* According to this principle, it was necessary only to consult Scripture without tradition and without the guidance of ecclesiastical decision, if one wanted to know the revealed truth. That is in fact impossible. To free the Bible, however, from this Protestant isolation, and to reincorporate it into the interpretative tradition of the Church, we need not empty the Bible of part of its revealed truth in order to justify the necessity of filling the ensuing gap with a supplemental oral tradition. The oral tradition and teaching of the Church are absolutely necessary for the knowledge of revelation, but not in the sense of imparting revealed truths handed down, so to speak, alongside the Bible. Tradition's function is to unfold and to explicate Scripture in the full depths of its content.

It has often been the practice, on the one hand, to regard Sacred Scripture and the teaching tradition of the Church as two parallel sources of truth from which we may learn what God has revealed to his Church. From this point of view some revealed doctrines are clearly enough found in Scripture, but others have entered into the Church's faith only in an oral tradition, as it were, bypassing Sacred Scripture. To justify this paralleling of Scripture and teaching tradition as two different sources of revelation, appeal is often made to the fact that there are dogmas that cannot be proved from the Bible. Upon closer examination, however, we see that the thrust of this argument could go against the users themselves. Taking these same dogmas, here presumed not provable from the Bible, is it possible then to *prove,* on the basis of oral tradition as we know it from the works of the Church Fathers, that these dogmas go back as far as the apostles? The immaculate

conception, for example, is not attested to until after
the first thousand years of Christianity; Mary's bodily
assumption into heaven is not attested to until the 6th
century. The necessity of baptism is, in the tradition of
the first two centuries, nowhere more expressly declared
than in Sacred Scripture. These are only a few of the
examples which show that something can belong to the
original revelation of the Lord even though it cannot
be proven by explicit testimony from an earlier time.
That it does belong to revelation testifies with clear
certainty to the teaching authority given the Church by
virtue of the promised guidance of the Holy Spirit. In
the original body of revelation, as the apostles and the
early Church proclaimed and believed it, these truths
are not expressly contained in so many statements, but
only implicitly and in a hidden way — so hidden under
certain circumstances that neither purely natural logic
nor interpretative skill but only the guidance of the
Holy Spirit can bring them to light. This holds true for
the oral tradition of apostolic times, just as much as it
does for Scripture. There are here no greater difficulties
for the entire revelation being potentially and essentially
contained in Scripture than there are for the oral tradition.

For something to be in Sacred Scripture or in oral
tradition, and for us to be able to prove it from these
sources, are not the same thing. Obviously one can
prove from a document only what is either expressly
contained in it, or can be inferred with the aid of purely
human logic, or explicated with the aid of natural
interpretation. If such possibilities for proof are lacking, this does not necessarily signify that a meaning is
not hidden in the depth of the text, a meaning that only
the Church with the supernatural guidance of the Holy
Spirit can render unambiguously clear. The guarantee is

given not to the individual person but to the teaching Church: what is proclaimed by her as God's revelation, really belongs to the depths of Scripture. With regard to this activity of the Church, the Council of Trent spoke explicitly of the "suggestion of the Holy Spirit", and the "dictates of the Holy Spirit" (Denz. 792a, 783).

Moreover, when Pius XII in his encyclical, *Humani generis* (1950), says that it is the task of theologians to show how the individual truths of the faith are contained in Scripture and in tradition as the two sources of faith, this does not necessarily mean that Scripture and tradition are parallel and unrelated sources, completely independent of one another. The theologian naturally has the task, after he has received an article of faith from the teaching Church, first of all to ask whether this truth cannot also be pointed out in the text of Scripture as it stands. He may indeed also point to tradition as a vessel of this evidence. This is to take tradition not as a stream that has flowed down to us alongside Scripture but rather in the sense of a unifying bond connecting, in a living process of interpretation, the Bible, which stands at the beginning, with the teaching Church today. Thus Scripture stands at the *beginning of the tradition of the Church,* just as the God-Man himself stood at the *beginning* of the preaching of the apostles.

Moreover, there are also weighty and positive reasons that cause us to regard the inspired biblical Word of God as a bearer of the entire divine revelation, at least in embryonic form. Admittedly, this revelation needs for its full explication the teaching of the Church, guided by the Holy Spirit.

The Catholic tradition — and its theology up to the time of the systematic textbooks of the late Middle Ages — has with remarkable explicitness regarded itself as primarily concerned with Sacred Scripture. Medieval theology speaks of itself as "the sacred page" (*sacra pagina*), using a name designating Scripture. Up until recent doctrinal pronouncements, in fact, the magisterium itself reflected the conviction that all the truths of the faith have their germinal source in Scripture. Why should the teaching Church, in every dogma that she defines, point to Scripture as at least the *ultimate foundation,* as is stated in the papal bull defining the bodily assumption of Mary into heaven? Why, if not from the conviction that nothing in the faith of the Church is unwritten, and that nothing besides Scripture could have been handed down through an oral tradition?

The dogma of inspiration itself, however, is the primary reason for the source of content for the teaching of the entire post-apostolic Church. In this teaching, Scripture is singled out from all other theological sources in a way explicable only if the Bible is the key starting point, the substance that tradition interprets. Certainly tradition has also attributed inspiration to general councils and has seen the "suggestion of the Holy Spirit" at work in them. The argument for this point of view, however, requires an essential distinction between the inspiration of Scripture, through which God himself becomes the author of the Bible, and the inspiration of the councils. Furthermore, it clarifies why the two are not simply parallel.

Scripture's Need of the Teaching Church

For its part, Sacred Scripture must have the interpretation of the teaching Church in order to do its work within the Church. Scripture lives, as God intended it to, only within the tradition of the Church as guided by the Holy Spirit. Paul warns us that "the letter kills, but the spirit gives life" (2 Cor. 3, 6; Rom. 2, 29; 7, 6). This substantiates the precise point being made here: Christianity is not a religion that has locked its faith within the dead vault of a written book. In this sense the letter of the Bible would kill. The Church finds life because the Spirit of God opens this vault, enabling the Church to live from its riches. However, the work of this Holy Spirit must not be misunderstood; it is not merely spiritual, as though the Spirit worked without embodiment and without organs. He is embodied in the organism of the Church. In her body of doctrine and faith he awakens the supernatural ingenuity that enables the Church to discover the hidden and deep meaning of Scripture on her journey through the centuries.

The reason why the Bible depends on the Church, whose life is from the Spirit of God, is not only the ambiguity of the biblical Word, resulting in a wide variety of interpretations among which the one true interpretation must be discovered. Inspiration itself absolutely requires the "suggesting" action of the Holy Spirit in the interpreting Church. The inspiration that produced the Bible did not see to it simply that the authors with the aid of the Holy Spirit wrote better and more correctly what they could also have written on their own. Inspiration can also — in the manner of the mystery of the God-Man himself — place a divine depth of meaning within the depth of the humanly grasped meaning; this can be hidden as well as presented in the humanly grasped word. Therefore the guidance of the Holy Spirit in the Church, as guaranteed by our Lord, must not only make the difficulties of the biblical text comprehensible and sort out its true meaning from its ambiguities. Rather, it is the function of the Spirit of God himself to draw from the depths of the text into the light of conscious belief those things that he himself has put into those depths by inspiration. It is possible with the human art of interpretation, although not always easy, to determine the substance and the spirit of the written words on a natural human level. Whether in this way we have arrived at the divine depth of meaning — the interconnections and perspectives intended by God — can only be ascertained "under the suggestion of the Holy Spirit" in the Church.

For this reason it is not possible for the teaching Church to prove this divine depth of meaning, which during the course of time she has increasingly brought to life from the texts, in the same sense that it is the ambition of science to demand proof. Sacred Scripture is not the kind of instrument or norm that might enable an individual to verify the Church's pronouncements. Consequently, it does seem astonishing at first that the teaching Church herself repeatedly directs people's attention away from the results of her scriptural exegesis and back to the written word of the Bible itself. It might seem that she intends here to show critics that her doctrine agrees with Scripture, as though to say: verify for yourself in the biblical Word the teaching I proclaim to you. However, this cannot be her intention. The connection between the Church's teachings and the biblical Word is guaranteed through the guidance of the Holy Spirit, even when this connection eludes human verification.

Whenever the teaching Church repeatedly refers us back to the biblical basis and starting point, what she testifies to is that she is not proclaiming her own word, but rather Christ, who stands with her at her very beginning. The apostles themselves based their preaching on the divine-human master himself, whose living preaching brought them revelation. When the Church as the body of Christ is given organized, institutional form, the divine-human source of the Church's faith also acquires institutional form in the "written Word of God", the Bible. The Church has this book so that she will always be conscious that it is Christ's Word and works she lives by. In her remembrance and reference to Scripture, the teaching Church cannot of course *prove* in all points that her proclamation comes from Christ. However, she can testify by reference to the Bible that she is proclaiming under the aegis of the Holy Spirit what has been handed down to her as the revealed words of Christ through the inspiration of the Holy Spirit.

We can sum up our discussion by saying that Scripture is the instrument which the inspiring God has given to his Church so that the faithful under her guidance may meditatively receive and prayerfully respond to God's revelation. Thus, Scripture is the instrument of living encounter between God and man. Because of inspiration, this instrument offers God's communication of himself to us without error. This truth without error, however, is found only if we seek to understand biblical utterances in the way they are intended to be understood. Clarity concerning the meaning of the Bible comes from the Holy Spirit himself through the teaching authority of the Church under his guidance. Scripture came into being through a special grace of God, permeating the depths of the physical and spiritual actions of the biblical writers and the depths of the historical processes that contributed to the development of the biblical books. The entire book, just as it is, carries divine inspiration within it in the way a human body contains its animating soul. The Bible is related to the Church's teaching as the living Christ is related to the preaching of the apostles: it is a starting point that gives the teaching its content. However, whatever content its words carry can only be brought to light through the working of the Holy Spirit himself within the teaching Church.

STUDY-CLUB QUESTIONS

1. What is the difficulty with regarding the Bible simply as a document of the origins of the Christian faith?

2. What is the value of a literary approach to the Bible? What is the difficulty?

3. How do the definitions of Trent and Vatican I on inspiration in Sacred Scripture differ from the later encyclicals of recent popes on Scripture? Do these two views contradict each other?

4. What two kinds of knowledge does the author distinguish, and on what basis?

5. What is meant by scriptural inerrancy? What happens when one gives undue emphasis to inerrancy as an effect of biblical inspiration? When is the effort to understand the Bible's content meaningful?

6. Considering that they wrote narratives of events that would represent the world in which they lived, how would you describe the approach of the biblical authors? What was their purpose? What

analogy does the author use to illustrate the biblical treatment of history?

7. If it is not important that we know whether God's inspiration affected one person or many, and whether it was active during a long series of centuries or not, what *are* we concerned with when considering how biblical inspiration occurred?

8. Since the Bible is inspired by God, can we take it literally in all its texts? Explain.

9. What is the Bible's place in the teaching of the Church? Explain. What is meant by the *Sola Scriptura* principle of the Reformation? Are Scripture and tradition two parallel sources of Christian revelation? To what extent are they related?

10. How is Scripture the instrument of *living* encounter between God and man?

II
What Is Faith?

Nature and Shape of Christian Belief

INTRODUCTION

I<small>T</small> is the mission of the Church through the centuries to present the work of Christ to mankind, for whose sake that work was accomplished. She should seek to bring mankind under the influence of Christ's salvation. Therefore her program is that of Christ, who proclaimed before Pilate: "This is why I was born, and why I have come into the world, to bear witness to the truth" (John 18, 37). Thus the Church, too, must bear witness to the truth and summon mankind to faith.

However, the Church must reckon with the fact that people will confront her with the same skeptical question that Pilate asked: "What is truth?" (John 18, 38). They may even concede that the witness of the Church must be understood "with faith". But since they do not impute to that "faith" the realism which they ascribe to truth, they reduce the teaching of the Church to mere myths and allegorical utterances. And so their faith becomes simply another way of asking the skeptical question: "But what is truth?"

In apparently trying to counteract this reduction of faith to hollow myth, others set forth a concept of faith that runs the risk of mistaking the witness of the Church for a mere communication of factual knowledge. They are too little aware that this truth must be lived. Their approach to the obligation of faith is too academic.

Even these few remarks clarify how important it is to study the nature and form of Christian faith. It is surely impossible to grasp faith through purely theoretical instruction; to be learned, this faith must also be lived. Because faith comes through personal decision, however, it cannot happen without personal knowledge of what is involved.

FAITH, WRONGLY UNDERSTOOD

The meaning of faith does not emerge from the usage of the word itself. In everyday use it has a wide variety of meanings and many of them are quite useless for understanding Christian faith. Moreover, these meanings constantly create so much confusion that we must clear them away right at the very beginning. Consequently, there is good reason for looking into two common misconceptions of faith, from which faith in the Christian sense essentially differs.

Faith as an Admission of Uncertainty

Actually we use the word *belief* (or believe) chiefly to express uncertainty about something. If we have no certain knowledge about a matter, or only suspect or vaguely remember that it is so, we say: I believe it is so. We have of course certain grounds for the correctness of our belief. We are aware when we make such a statement that it has some degree of contact with reality, but this contact is not altogether firm. Our assertion is based largely on combinations of elements which for the most part our own thought processes have "filled in" as supplements to the bare outline of what was actually observed. And so, if we are honest, we do not make categorical statements on the basis of such supplementary (and therefore possibly erroneous) elements; instead, we express a *belief* as to what happened. Depending on the circumstances, this belief might be variously expressed as "I *think* so," "I *presume* so," "I feel," "It is my opinion that," or some other qualifying statements that more or less reflect our subjective frame of mind regarding the facts. Belief of this sort, however, is not of much value in shaping and giving direction to one's life. For that it is necessary to see reality as clearly as possible and to take it fully into account.

The uncertainty described above, however, is the very thing that distinguishes this "opinion" or "belief" from religious faith in the Catholic sense. Religious faith, as meant by the Church, supersedes all other affirmations by virtue of its guarantee of certainty stemming from God's infallibility. Where this faith is genuinely involved, it is the most certain and most reliable declaration available to man. Only one very remote similarity between "faith" in the everyday sense (as a synonym for "belief" or "opinion") and faith in the religious sense can explain why the same word is used for two such different realities: in both instances the certainty involved is not based solely on human perception. In the area of opinion, this incompleteness of human perception and evidence ultimately acts only to destroy any certainty. In the area of a religious faith based on God's revelation, on the other hand, certainty is deepened and enhanced, because its foundation is not human insight but rather the infallible authority of the revealing God. Thus the slight similarity between the two kinds of belief involves at the same time their greatest dissimilarity.

Faith as an Abandonment of All Claim to Truth

The second misconception, from which we must carefully distinguish real faith, is to be found not so much in the everyday use of language as in the statement of fundamental positions on questions of philosophy. This misconception can take a number of different forms, but all of them basically imply an attitude of resignation about finding an answer that could satisfy the human search for the ultimate and deepest reasons for our existence. We know that an answer to the questions of the origin, direction, and real meaning of human existence is the prerequisite for fashioning our lives in a way worthy of a human being. Of course there are many who live out their lives apparently without any concern for a possible underlying meaning. Some even consider the persistent search for an answer to the "why" of life to be a kind of infantile sickness. In reality, however, the seemingly endless question of "why", with which children plague and frequently embarrass their parents, represents the first awakening of the conscious life of the human being. It may be that the adolescent temporarily thrusts such a question into the background in his zest for life and in the full awareness of his vital energies. Upon reaching adulthood, however, man is again confronted with the urgency of this question. In fact, many of the psychoses suffered by modern man stem from the fact that this question, either because of fear of the answer or inability to answer, is repressed in the depths of the unconscious and causes psychic disturbance.

On the one hand, then, this question about ultimates demands an answer; on the other hand, the opinion is widely held that the mind cannot find a satisfying and certain answer beyond the realm of immediate experience. Then the attempt is made to resolve this dilemma by looking for some means other than the human mind to satisfy this urge to question. This answer, provided not by the mind receptive to truth but by some other human means, is given the name of "faith". This faith is not supposed to involve the mind, nor is its object really truth or reality. Rather, the description of such a faith goes something like this: the question of the origin and destiny of man, the question of God and human conduct toward him — questions, therefore, of a religious nature — can be answered only by means of human experience, by a certain feeling of dependence on the Almighty. In a word, such questions can only be answered in terms of *emotion*.

Another aspect of such a faith holds that it is the will's free decision that provides everyday human existence with a "background", a philosophy of life, or a religion: whatever we call it, clearly it can make no claim to truth. It is only the decision of the human will that gives underlying meaning to the actions of everyday human life. Such a religion, such a faith, has no intention of being accepted as truth, but at the very most can be only a symbolic expression of what is indeed conceded to be a divine depth of meaning lying beyond all things. Yet the truth of this meaning — it is resignedly confessed — must remain forever obscure to human experience.

This misconception of faith likewise bears only a

slight resemblance to faith as the Church understands it. The resemblance may be seen in the fact that in the Catholic sense of faith the decision of the human will plays an important, indeed a determining, role. In addition, faith has an influence on the emotions, and the emotions in turn can be a factor in bringing about faith. A one-sided approach to Christian faith, as if it were a matter only of the mind, is no more justifiable than making faith an emotional experience or merely a decision of the will. As Schnackenburg says: "Both extremes are . . . to be avoided, an excessive emphasis on the emotional factors . . . or the one-sided over-estimate of that rational conviction, which mistrusts all those psychological and frequently imponderable forces that alone make faith capable of living warmth and bring it to full growth" (*The Moral Teaching of the New Testament,* New York, 1965, p. 39).

However, the act of faith, in the immediate and proper sense, proceeds from the human mind, which in faith grasps reality as truth. Of course, in order that the mind may do this, may give its intellectual assent to reality, there must be a free decision of the human will sustained by grace. This, however, is entirely different from that so-called faith which abandons hope of finding a clear answer to the deepest questions of the thirsting human spirit and attempts to assuage that thirst by emotional experience or by the will's edict.

UNDERSTANDING FAITH FROM HOLY SCRIPTURE

By clearly contrasting all the misconceptions of faith with the meaning of faith as found in divine revelation and the teaching of the Church, we find ourselves at first in a somewhat embarrassing position. Whoever seeks a Christian understanding of faith will look with good reason where he will encounter Christ and his Word — in Sacred Scripture. He will believe that Christ and his truth, and therefore the divine words of Sacred Scripture itself, have been sustained by the Church through the centuries and first brought to fruition in the life of the Church. Therefore he will ask this Church herself what she proclaims concerning the nature and form of faith. However, here we perhaps unexpectedly notice that the two sources, the Bible and the teaching Church, seem to give quite different interpretations of what Christian faith is. Scripture seems to envision a faith of far more fullness and vitality than does the interpretation set forth by the teaching Church. In what follows we intend first of all to compare these two interpretations of the faith. The difference that emerges from such a comparison may at first strike us as something of a problem. Yet that will prepare us to look for the overall view, in which both interpretations become a unity and show us the total reality of the faith. We shall speak of this total reality in our final summary.

Sacred Scripture does indeed afford us a view of faith in its living and full actuality. Let us try to single out the most important elements in the biblical view of the structure of faith.

Man's Openness to the Call of God

According to Scripture, faith is actually the comprehensive term for that general human attitude that responds to the call of the divine Lord and to him alone. Faith is the attitude and direction of life to which man should become converted. This is emphasized at the beginning of New Testament preaching and permeates its entire content. John the Baptist prepares man for the coming of Christ by a call to repentance and conversion (Matt. 3, 2). Christ himself appropriates this sermon of his forerunner (Mark 1, 15) and at the same time proclaims himself the goal of this repentance (Matt. 11, 28). For this reason the Church also must begin her teaching with this admonition to repent (Acts 2, 38). This somewhat more negative conception of conversion—turning away from former attitudes—ends in faith as its positive counterpart. Thus the biblical concept of faith is as comprehensive as the concept of metanoia, which means a conversion of the total person with all his human powers and talents.

According to Scripture, faith means the attitude in which man opens himself to the challenging call of God and lets himself be guided by that call. Thus in the New Testament faith always means obedience to God. Saint Paul, particularly, associates obedience with a faithful listening to God's Word. The faith of which Abraham was a particularly outstanding example, the faith through which justification came, is a hearing of God's Word of truth that comes as a divine guidance to which man must be obedient (Rom. 4). The letter to the Hebrews also speaks of the just men of the Old Testament, who pleased God because of their faith. This faith, however, was obedience (Heb. 11). With Paul this faith and obedience coalesce into one concept of faithful obedience (Rom. 1, 5; 16, 26). According to St. Peter, it is in obedience that one receives the truth (1 Pet. 1, 22). Obedience, however, is a quality that determines a person's total attitude. Thus an entire life can be fashioned from faith, and faith proves to be the all-encompassing defining quality of an entire personality. According to Weiser, even in the Old Testament "faith is a relationship to God which embraces the entire person in the totality of his outward behavior and his interior life" (TWNT 6, p. 188).

This comprehensive understanding of faith as a person's general attitude, open to the divine call, contains various elements. These correspond to the various aspects of the personal life of man. Thus in the scriptural concept of faith we may find one element that emphasizes human understanding and another element that emphasizes the right disposition of the will.

Faith in the Truth of God's Word

The metanoia in which man is converted to faith is, of course, the complete conversion (metanoia) of the total person together with all of his powers. And yet inherent in the very word itself there is already a clear suggestion of an intellectual element that concerns the human mind: metanoia literally means "rethinking". The biblical concept of faith is similar to this. As comprehensive and total in its emphasis as it is, yet the first of its elements is an intellectual one. It is a faith that first of all gives credence to words which are received as true. For how could we obey words whose content we did not accept as reality?

When, for example, we read that after the resurrection of the Lord the disciples "believed the Scripture and the Word which Jesus had spoken", because they remembered from their experience of the risen Lord that he had spoken of it earlier, then here we are clearly dealing with faith in the sense of acceptance-as-true, in the sense therefore of an act of the mind. In response to the spoken word, assent is given to a reality expressed by that word. When Paul in his trial before Felix, the governor of Caesarea, confesses that he believed "all things that are written in the Law and the prophets" (Acts 24, 14), then he confesses to a "teaching", which is first affirmed by the believing mind. Thus also Christ reproaches the disciples for their slowness to "believe in all that the prophets have spoken" (Luke 24, 25). The Lord explains the fact that the Jews did not believe in him by saying that they did not believe the writings of Moses either (John 5, 46f.).

Not only must credence be given to the revealed Word of God laid down in the Old Testament; it must also be given to the Word that he sends here and now to mankind through his angel. This distinguishes the faith of Mary (Luke 1, 45) from the disbelief of Zacharias (Luke 1, 20). Wherever the New Testament concept of faith is to a certain extent defined there is to be sure always an element of trust involved, and there is also clear evidence of that intellectual element which relates faith to knowledge: "Now faith is the substance of things hoped for, the evidence of things that are not seen ... By faith we understand that the world was fashioned by the Word of God" (Heb. 11, 1. 3).

Confident Surrender to the God We Trust

The text just cited leads us to the element in the will's disposition that is foremost in the biblical conception of faith — confidence, or trust. Man is able to willingly listen to the call of God and follow this call obediently when, like Abraham who left his homeland, he puts his trust in God (Rom. 4, 16-21). Even in the

Old Testament, faith is always an act of the trusting will striving for a hoped-for good. However, the New Testament also always shows faith as being characterized by the power of trust. Whenever Christ demands "faith" of those who come to him seeking healing and help, he seems to mean confidence and trust much more than an intellectual assent to a truth. Jesus verifies that it was faith which helped the woman who, pronounced incurable by the physicians, was restored to health by touching the hem of Jesus' robe (Luke 8, 48), and that it was also faith which saved the sinful woman, full of loving trust, who bathed the feet of the master in fragrant oils in the house of the Pharisee (Luke 7, 50). Jesus reawakens hope in the ruler of the synagogue by telling him, after his daughter had died: "Do not be afraid; only have faith and she shall be saved" (Luke 8, 50). The Canaanite woman, whose importunities could not be stilled by the reminder that she was not of the chosen people, was assured: "O woman, great is thy faith!" (Matt. 15, 28). All of these incidents indicate a recognition of the trust with which these people hoped for help; the same is true for many other scriptural passages. Faith as an assent of the intellect to truth seems here, though not denied, still not the most important thing. The faith that moves mountains is quite clearly faith in its aspect of trust (Mark 11, 23f.). This definition of faith as trusting devotion is confirmed in a negative way when the Lord reproaches the disciples for their little faith, which really appears as a lack of trust (Matt. 6, 30; 8, 26 ; 14, 31; 16, 8).

This understanding of faith corresponds to what the Bible means by God's truth and trustworthiness. The Old Testament in particular, whenever it speaks of God's truth and reliability, means primarily his standing by his promised Word — something we would call loyalty. This reliability, however, is precisely what sustains faith as trust and confidence.

Receiving the Message of Christ

Therefore, as presented to us in Sacred Scripture, faith emerges as a very vital reality giving definition to the life of man. This is true not only of faith as human attitude and human action; it is also true of the content of this faith. It is not an abstract theological truth and utterance about God; rather, it is God himself, to the degree that we encounter him in Christ. It has been said that the specifically Christian understanding of faith is found in faith as the acceptance of the message of Christ. In this is expressed both the character of faith as it gives direction to the whole man as well as its uniqueness in realizing the personal encounter with God. Our personal encounter with God is made possible and takes place in faith through revelation and grace. God sent his Son in our human nature in order that we might see in a tangible and bodily form the otherwise invisible, and therefore remote, God. He was sent that we bodily beings might meet him personally. The God-Man is the image of the invisible God (Col. 1, 15). In him the invisible God becomes perceptible to our senses. After Christ has ascended into the invisible heavens beyond, he is presented to each individual by the message of the Church. Man must receive the message of Christ, the incarnate Word of God, and from it nourish an attitude of devotion, faith, obedience and trust that will govern his entire life. This is the scriptural process of faith.

FAITH IN CATHOLIC THEOLOGICAL THOUGHT

The function of the theologian is to ponder deeply

about, and understand more clearly, what has been handed down through the centuries in the form of the Bible and tradition as the revelation of God. If the results of this process are valid, they must not contradict the meaning of Scripture. Since theology, however, is the thoughtful penetration not only of an oral body of tradition but also of the revealed Word of God as written in the Bible, it is inevitable that we find the vital elements of Scripture reflected in this theology. Consequently, what we have learned of Catholic faith from the Bible is bound to be given clearer definition in what Catholic theology has to say about faith; certainly the structure of faith will be more sharply delineated.

The results of theological endeavors to understand what is meant by faith were given rather definitive form by Vatican I in 1869. There faith was defined as "supernatural virtue, by which, with the inspiration and help of God's grace, we believe that what he has revealed is true, not because its intrinsic truth is seen with the natural light of reason, but because of the authority of God who reveals it, of God who can neither deceive nor be deceived" (Denz. 1789).

Grasping the Truth

What is affirmed here is a reality which exists before the human person believes in it and which would continue to exist even if that person refused to believe in it. In faith, the human being appropriates this reality to himself in an interior way. The mind of a person makes inward statements, so to speak, about outward reality. If what the mind affirms is in accord with objective reality, we then call this state of affairs truth. Verification of the truth of our faith belongs, however, essentially to the Church.

Thus faith is here related to knowledge. "By faith we understand . . ." (Heb. 11, 3). Like knowledge, faith also is the comprehension of reality by the human mind. Faith and knowledge, however, are distinct from each other in the way in which they grasp reality and in the different spheres of reality to which they relate. We shall speak of these distinctions shortly.

In this relationship of faith and knowledge, in their common purpose of grasping reality, we encounter familiar difficulties. There is found either a tension between faith and knowledge, or a contradiction between the two. If faith were any of those things we found ourselves compelled to reject at the very outset of this discussion, there would be no problem. Faith and knowledge could say opposite things without cancelling one another out. They would be operating on completely different levels. Since in fact they do share a common level of function — that of comprehending reality — we cannot be content with a contradiction between them. Two statements that are true cannot contradict one another. If science has learned that the earth revolves about the sun, then faith cannot say that the earth is the center of the universe, at least not in any physical sense. Faith and knowledge must be taken with equal seriousness because of the obligation that reality imposes on the human mind. That is why we are so disturbed when faith and knowledge make contradictory statements. For this can only mean either that scientific research has gone wrong or that what was taken as revelation actually is not. Both approaches to reality seek certainty — through further inquiry in the field of knowledge and through further search for the true meaning of revelation in the area of

faith. In the final analysis revelation must be safe-
guarded by the teaching Church by virtue of the infallibility conferred on her by God.

Revealed Reality

Faith and knowledge, we found, are related in terms
of their common purpose of discerning reality. However, as indicated earlier, we shall find that they are
quite different — both as to the source of the reality to
be perceived and as to the motive for the mind's assent
to reality. In knowledge, the intellect perceives reality
because the reality is readily accessible to the view and
grasp of the mind. The mind of the perceiver assimilates
the reality immediately confronting it. This is appropriate for the responsibility God gave to man at creation to subdue the earth (Gen. 1, 28). Man's naming
of the animals (Gen. 2, 19f.) is a symbol of his perception and subjugation of reality.

Faith, on the other hand, gives its assent to reality
because reality is presented to it through the free revelation of God. Above and beyond knowledge — in which
man explores the empirical realm and even to some
degree penetrates the underlying principles of the meta-
physical by dint of his own mental efforts — there are
realms not accessible to natural human reason. They
constitute mystery. If the human mind is also to learn
something about these areas of reality, then God himself must impart such knowledge. "We speak of what
we know, and bear witness to what we have seen," says
Jesus to Nicodemus. From this need for an eyewitness,
he proves that we must pay heed to him as the only
eyewitness to the things of the beyond: "No one has
ascended into heaven." No human being was ever in

heaven and descended from heaven and therefore able to speak as an eyewitness except . . . the Son of Man (John 3, 11-13). Even before the time of Christ, through his revealed Word, God had already made known to man the depths of the reality that man's mind could not have perceived through its own powers. This self-revelation of God to man reached its culmination when the Son of God visibly entered our history as a man and told us of the mysteries of God. "God, who at sundry times and in divers manners spoke in times past to the fathers by the prophets, last of all in these days has spoken to us by his Son" (Heb. 1, 1f.).

To that extent, therefore, the relation between faith and knowledge is qualified; a difference in their subject matter is also established. Why did God reveal a reality that would otherwise be hidden from our minds? This happened because God wanted human beings to share in the life of a reality that is more than natural human existence and is, therefore, supernatural. This reality, which we call grace, is a participation in that living community that exists between Father, Son and Holy Spirit in the triune God. The Son of God came to us men and bound us closely to himself so that the same life, in which he is one with the Father and the Holy Spirit, might be ours to share with the triune God. We can receive this sharing in the life of God only as a gift. We cannot achieve it by our power. Nevertheless we must receive this life through our own personal decision and realize it through our own personal efforts. The life of grace is the life of Christ and it should be lived as our own. However, that entails knowing in some sense what is involved. What we do not know about, we cannot achieve by personal decision. Therefore God has shown to us the works of his grace in human history and has given us the reality of this grace through his revealed Word. If we accept this Word in faith, we may not be able to penetrate and fully understand what we have been given, but we can make a personal decision in response to a personal gift intended for us.

From what has gone before we see that, despite the kinship between faith and knowledge, there are essential differences between them. Faith is associated with a reality revealed by God "which completely transcends the human mind" (Denz. 1786). Knowledge, on the other hand, is associated with the facets of reality that are open to the inquiring human mind. There are occasions when the revealing Word of God reaches into even these regions, "which are by their nature accessible to human reason" (Denz. 1786). Since God does enter by his saving grace into human history, he cannot bring revelation without also affecting these natural areas. Such realities — for example, that the human soul is a spirit and immortal and cannot have developed from matter — can then become objects of scientific knowledge and at the same time also be matters of faith, i.e., be accepted on the authority of the revealing God. To the extent that human knowledge has not failed through error, however, it is never rendered invalid by faith or by the revelation of God. Knowledge is just extended to a new depth with which it was in fact always compatible — but not recognized by the mind — until the mind affirmed in faith what God revealed concerning that knowledge.

Connected with both these differences between faith and knowledge — difference in motives impelling the mind's consent to comprehended reality, and difference in areas of reality comprehended — there is yet a third difference between the two. When the human mind is confronted with a reality that it perceives directly or by the effort of its thought, then it is no longer possible for it to "lock out" this reality, so to speak. The existence of the reality must be admitted, and there is no longer any freedom to deny it. The situation is quite different with the reality that can enter the human mind only through divine revelation, and hence is perceived in faith. Divine revelation indeed testifies to a reality, but it does not directly submit this reality to human perception; nor does it proceed through intellectual insight. When a person makes an honest and strenuous mental effort to comprehend God's revelation, he can reach the point where his insight will tell him: I am now obliged to believe, because it is God who has spoken. Here, too, there is a "must" involved, but it is a "must" of quite a different kind from the "must" that compels the mind by direct observation or reasoned inference. That is a physical, "it-cannot-be-otherwise" situation, but the "must" which urges faith is a moral obligation. It appeals to the free decision of the human person. Therefore faith, much more immediately than knowledge, involves personal encounter with God and a surrender to him in acknowledgment of his authority. When a person says: "I believe in this truth," then of course the content of the truth is implicit in such belief. However, there is much more involved, for here a meeting has occurred between the revealing God and the believing person, and they have met on the common ground of the truth that is the content of revelation.

The Intellect, the Will and Grace

This quality of faith as a free moral decision of a person before God leads us to a third question. Freedom is not an attribute of the intellect, but of the will. Up to now, however, it has seemed as if the intellect were the sustaining factor in the act of faith. What actually are the forces that enable a person to carry out an act of faith?

If faith is the assimilation of reality as truth, then the power appropriate to it is the intellect, for the intellect enters into a relationship with truth. The intellect is that narrower region within the human spirit in which the act of faith has its roots; it is the unique faculty by whose power man's spirit is directed toward the assent of faith.

However, as we saw, the intellect through its own power can at best come only to the point of saying: "I am now obliged to give assent." For this obligation to be translated into action, an impetus is needed from that other power to which the moral realm is entrusted — the will. The obscurity of the mystery in which the reality is enshrouded causes the human intellect to shrink from its assent, despite the revelation of God. The decision of the will must move the intellect past this stumbling block. Faith is a moral act whose rationality and obligation the intellect may well perceive. For this act to occur, however, it is necessary that the will yield to the revealing God and, in so doing, move the intellect to acceptance.

Even the act of intellectual acceptance, moved by free will, cannot alone achieve real faith, for faith transcends natural powers. To man revealed truth is strange because it puts a restraint on that self-assurance with which he would like to investigate all reality on his own. Even if man were capable of comprehending revealed truths by his own power, such power would still not be sufficient for genuine faith. God intends faith to be a living act, partaking of that divine quality to which man must be inwardly raised through God's grace. The life of Christ, entering into a human being as grace, brings possibilities for faith that far transcend human reckoning. When those who proclaim the faith become disheartened at times and feel as though all their efforts are meaningless and in vain in a world that is materialistic, secular and no doubt even diabolically disposed — even then faith endures and remains alive, defying all human explanation.

THE TOTAL REALITY OF FAITH

The Question

Faith was represented to us in the Bible as a living complex of forces shaping all human life. In this complex, however, we found the basic element to be an assent to truth by the human intellect. In the conception of faith developed by Catholic theology and defined by Vatican I, this intellectual element is undoubtedly in the foreground, even though our attention is directed toward a region beyond merely intellectual powers. Vatican I characterized faith as "full submission of the intellect and will to the revealing God" (Denz. 1789). There can be no doubt that the above two aspects of faith belong together. Yet *how* are they related? Does faith as defined by Vatican I constitute only a part of what faith is according to Scripture? If so, it is difficult to understand why only this partial element is called faith, as if it comprised the entire reality implicitly in the word. Or did Vatican I really intend to encompass the full nature of that reality with its definition? In that case it would require an explanation as to how the much more comprehensive and complex reality, referred to in Scripture as "faith" and discussed in the earlier part of this study, could bear that same label and, further, just how that label is to be understood.

Actually, "faith" can be understood in two ways: in its essential and more restricted sense, and in its wider and more complex sense. The first denotes the nature or essence of faith as a nucleus underlying the various personal forces and actions permeated by it. The second refers to the full concrete reality of those forces and actions whose underlying motive is intellectual assent to faith. Since in reality this "nuclear" act of faith will always be manifest in terms of complex life situations, it is quite understandable how the word "faith" acquires its double use. In theological discussion it will tend to acquire its narrower and more essential meaning; in an account of human actions — such as we find in Scripture — "faith" will more often refer, by a natural derivation from its essential meaning, to the entire complex of deeds and events that it informs.

The connection between faith in its narrower sense and faith in the wider sense, that is, in the sense of its existence within a living totality, is twofold.

Faith as Encounter

Man is not to give assent in faith to the revelation of God merely in order to enrich his knowledge. Human knowledge is in fact expanded beyond its natural bounds by God's message to man. However, God does not reveal himself for academic purposes but for the sake of a living communion with man. "Now this is everlasting life, that they may know thee, the only true God, and him whom thou hast sent, Jesus Christ" (John 17, 3). The life of grace is designated as the knowledge that brings God and man together in personal encounter through the mediation of Christ, who is both God and man. This knowledge, made possible by Christ's revelation, can also *become* life, a living communion with God in personal encounter, and through this communion, can become a union of grace with him. Such knowledge, however, is the faith of which we speak.

If this faith is to be a personal encounter with the self-revealing God, it must begin with the perception of truth. In order that man may meet him, the infinite God must reveal himself as truth to man, for truth is the core of living encounter. In this encounter, however, the living God calls to man, and man makes a personal response in faith to God's call. Whenever a person gives his intellect over to God's revealed truth, the entire life of that person is set in motion. Only when the total person, with all of his powers, surrenders himself completely to this truth, is his intellect able to perceive God's revealed reality as truth.

Thus it is not so remarkable that the word "faith" is used to refer both to this total activation of the life of the believer and, in a narrower sense, to the realm of the intellect. In Scripture, this intellectual function is only occasionally evident. For the most part the Bible uses the word "faith" to describe the encounter of the total person with God. There it is made clear that acceptance of truth by the intellect is only the nucleus of the larger surrender, and that intellectual assent is subordinate to personal encounter between man and the revealing God who summons him. The science of theology, on the other hand, calls our attention primarily to that intellectual nucleus. In so doing, it does not deny the living totality in which this nucleus lives and gives its assent. Theology is mainly concerned with explaining the narrower function of what constitutes the act of faith.

New Life through Faith

Whenever a person assents to the truth of what God has revealed, such assent, if genuine, will become evident in a totally new orientation of his life. God's revelation is not intended as mere theoretical knowledge. It discloses to our view realities that make demands on us. God reveals himself as an active God. His *Word* of revelation does not exist for its own sake, but is always accompanied by the *dynamic* of his salvation, just as a lover shows love in action as well as word. Therefore, a person's affirmation in faith must not remain on the level of mere intellectual assent, but must find expression in the active response of his life to God. Only then is man's faith adequate to God's revealed Word. When Scripture says: "He who is just lives by faith" (Rom. 1, 17; Gal. 3, 11), this means first of all the life of "righteousness", the state of grace attained by a person through faith, a justification by faith (Rom. 3, 28). In these words, however, there is a note of caution: the justification which God gives to us demands that our lives be refashioned through faith.

And so once again it should not seem strange to us when the Bible uses the word "faith" to mean total human life as refashioned by faith. This fullness of life evolves from the assent of the intellect that gives credence to the Word of revelation and accepts it as true. Faith as a total way of life before God no more contradicts faith as an assent of the mind to revealed truth than do Paul and James contradict one another when Paul says man is justified by faith (Rom. 3, 28), and James says faith apart from works is dead (James 2, 14-26). St. Paul can very rightly say of that faith, which he understands as the fullness of a life fashioned in faith, that it will bring justification from God. On the other hand, St. James must say, of faith understood in the narrower sense of intellectual assent to revealed truth, that it must be "completed by works" (James 2, 22). What really matters, as St. Paul tells us, is a "faith which works through charity" (Gal. 5, 6).

STUDY-CLUB QUESTIONS

1. What are two common misconceptions of faith?
2. What are the most important elements in the biblical view of the structure of faith? Which is foremost?
3. What is meant by metanoia? How is it related to faith?
4. In the New Testament, is faith understood primarily as an assent of the intellect to truth? Explain.
5. What is the specifically Christian understanding of faith?
6. How is faith related to knowledge? What are the difficulties here? What are the differences?
7. How is faith characterized in the Vatican I definition of 1869?
8. What does the science of theology stress in its understanding of faith? Does this seem to contradict the biblical understanding?

9. Explain the relationship between man's assent in faith to the revelation of God and man's living communion with God in a personal encounter.

10. How can we reconcile the seemingly contradictory statements about faith made by Paul and James in the New Testament?

III
Why the Church?

What the Catholic Church
Claims and What She Is

INTRODUCTION

To deny the existence of a sense of religion in everyone who happens to be outside the Church is wrong. Equally misguided and far more widespread is the opposite view that genuine religiousness is incompatible with life in the Church. This view misunderstands the nature of an institution which, like Christ himself, must put the challenging question: "Who do men say that I am?" (cf. Matt. 16, 13). Usually the answer is: "Some say this, some say that." Then comes the crucial question: "But *you,* who do you say that I am?" This question is directed to the faithful and sets them apart from those who do not believe.

THE CHURCH AS A PROBLEM

Why the Church? This question is neither meant rhetorically — as if asked by someone who, in unshaken confidence, does not see the Church as really a problem at all — nor is it meant merely in a didactic way — as if to urge us, or others, to deeper reflection concerning a Church that is all too often taken as something self-evident. Rather, this question is one that forces itself upon our attention, and if we ourselves are not aware of it, we shall surely hear it asked by our fellowmen.

Religion as an Inner Experience

Here we are confronted with a point of view that, during the course of human history, has frequently had great persuasive power. During times when worldliness tends to invade even the Church, provoking a counter tendency toward interiority, it is precisely people who are vitally religious that are tempted to set up a dichotomy between religion and Church. Religion does seem to be essentially a thing of the *spirit,* of an invisible *interiority*. It seems to be most at home in the quiet hidden recesses of the human soul, where it would still be invisible to anyone happening to disturb those recesses.

This spiritualism is by no means simply the refuge of those who would protect their religion from the attack of forces hostile to it or from the scorn of an uncomprehending world, and who therefore retreat into a realm of pure inwardness that makes no demands on them. The real problem arises for the Church when this view is based on the conviction that a *legally* organized Church, and therefore one that is externally manifest, somehow contradicts genuine religion as interiority. Often the more genuinely, and therefore interiorly, religious a person is, the more he feels compelled to dissociate himself from the visibly organized, and therefore outwardly manifest, Church. At the very most he may claim that the real nature of the Church is to be found only in those hidden depths of the spirit where man is united with God in true holiness and inward grace.

Religion as a Private Affair

Possibly just as ruinous for the Church is another seeming contradiction, which is connected for the most part with the misunderstood interiority mentioned above. If it were really essential for religion to remain hidden within the depths of the soul, then naturally it could only be of concern to the *individual*. Even if it is conceded that religion must be given outward expression, there is still a strong tendency to keep it as the preserve of the individual. In an age when tolerance is a watchword, the privacy of religion is quickly accepted as the easy solution; it must be left to each individual as to whether and in what way he is to be religious.

However, this attitude does not proceed solely from a desire for a nice, convenient situation in which a person can still be religious while nevertheless foregoing *community* obligations. Rather, this danger of individualism is inherent almost in the very nature of religious endeavor. For God, whom the religious person encounters, is actually the "Father who sees in secret" (Matt. 6, 4. 18); man knows that divine omniscience follows him even to the darkest depths of the earth (Psalm 139), and that he can rely on God as his only just judge even when condemned in the eyes of the world (Dan. 13, 42f.; 1 Cor. 4, 4). What wonder then, if the religious person tries to hide his meeting with God from an often unjust public scrutiny and to have this all to himself, perhaps as the only personal and private area left to him in a life that has been emptied of mystery?

In this view the Church necessarily becomes a problem. In the Church, religious life does appear to be removed from the *personal* realm and exposed to the light of a *public* society. Personal devotion to God seems to be changed into an official act of unconcealed worship. Even the very secret acts of penance and conversion appear to be subject to the legal stipulations of an organized society. This all has the appearance of an insoluble dilemma — at least when religion is so exclusively regarded as an *individual* matter that its social expression is considered to be out of the question, or so exclusively regarded as a matter of the *Church* that religion loses every bit of its private, interior and personal character. Both positions, however, would be equally false.

Religion as Free Decision

We come to a final question concerning the Church. The question remains even if it is conceded that man must be religious not only in his spiritual interiority but also in his bodily being, not only as a private individual but also in the open forum of human society. The question is whether this religious community of persons can be realized only in *one* form and find expression only in *one* unique fellowship. The concrete Church, however, with whom we are concerned here, calls herself Catholic also because she believes herself to have been founded as the sole legitimate religious community for all mankind.

There are three ways of trying to reconcile the necessity of the Church with the demands of individual

freedom of decision. We shall first examine these points
of view.

A Community of Persons

The first view sees the *ecclesia,* as Christ intended it
according to the New Testament, as purely a community of persons. That is to say, Christ sent forth his
call to each individual, and each individual who associated himself with Jesus did so on the basis of his
personal decision. Out of this aggregate of individual
decisions there arose that community which the New
Testament calls the *ecclesia.* This is the view of a number of non-Catholic theologians. Moreover, through the
centuries this community of persons of the Christian
religion was able to renew itself: attracted by the person of Christ, or perhaps even influenced by the sur-
rounding culture or urged on by religious need, the
individual person would make the decision to live a
Christian life. And since many do this, the community
of like-minded, namely Christian-minded, persons is
constantly formed anew. In this view, an organized
Church is by no means necessary.

Man-made Forms of Organization

Another view concedes that a vital Christian community of believers requires a certain fixity and organization. The concrete *form* of such a communal arrangement, however, is considered to be a purely human
structure, developed during the course of the centuries
and frequently altered. There are many such forms.
Which one of these the individual will belong to is left

to his choice, or depends on the circumstances that led him to this particular community, or on his family traditions, among which may be a particular form of religion that he chooses to follow.

"Tolerance"

The third view even concedes that Christ himself established a unique Church, which would therefore necessarily define the belief of her present-day members. Since we do in fact encounter a multitude of different Churches, the tolerant person of today will not acknowledge that one Church should maintain to the exclusion of others that *she* is the Church established by Christ. Rather, they should all concede the "wisdom" of the parable of the rings told by Lessing's Nathan, the point of which seems to eradicate all intolerance and to secure religious peace: *the genuine ring was presumably lost.*

Still, none of these views disposes of our Church as she understands herself, for associated with her is the claim to absoluteness, based on the conviction that she was *founded* by *Christ himself.* For many people today, however, who make all values relative and see all power as derived from human beings on up, such a claim makes the Church even more incomprehensible.

WHY THE CHURCH?

When we try to explain why there is a Church, we are not actually concerned so much with an *analysis of differences* that would seek to determine among the various Christian communions the Church which was established by Christ. Rather, we are here asking the much more fundamental question of *whether and why there is a Church-oriented religiousness at all.* Only when this question is answered is there any point to the further question of the true Church founded by Christ.

In the final analysis, the believing Christian belongs to his Church because *Christ established it* (Matt. 16, 17-19). Because Christ called the Church into being with the guarantee of her enduring to "the consummation of the world" (Matt. 28, 20), the believer partakes of the life of this Church so that he may live under the guidance of Christ. And yet, even if we do not share the opinion of many a modern that Christ did not really establish an ecclesiastical organization, we may further ask, indeed we must ask, *why* the Lord founded the Church at all. In asking such a question there need be no fear of departing from true allegiance to the faith because of some supposed need for our independently establishing the reasonableness of Christ's act. This is not the purpose of our question. Rather, it is to understand faith in its true depth that we examine revealed doctrine and Christ's order in establishing a Church.

Our point of departure will be two basic statements concerning Christ's work of redemption.

1. THE WHOLE MAN IS REDEEMED

First of all, we are concerned with the extent of Christ's redemption. The answer to this problem is not quite as obvious as it may seem. Everyone knows that it is the human person who is redeemed. The words, "Who for us men and for our salvation came down from heaven," have been uttered by the Church for centuries in the Creed. This human person, however, is not understood in his totality, as he ought to be if we really think of his salvation in its fullest sense. When Christ gives man salvation, or wholeness, through his work of redemption, then that is a supernatural gift of grace, far transcending human nature. We must recognize that this supernatural salvation redeems and saves the whole man. But what constitutes the whole man? Certainly, today we agree that not only the soul but also the body is meant. The dogma of the bodily assumption of Mary into heaven reminds us that the body is included in the glory of redemption. Even body and soul, however, still do not define the total actual existence of man.

We must consider that it is not the *abstract* nature of man that is redeemed, defined by the ancient philosophers as "animal rationale" (a living creature endowed with a mind). The human person cannot be redeemed until he actually *exists*. The sin from which Christ has redeemed us humans is, after all, something that really does befall us, whether it be the sin of Adam, which resides in us as an inherited fault, or whether it be our own sins, which burden us with personal guilt. The divine life through which Christ overcomes sin in us is a reality that can be present only in a person who exists.

Therefore, when we ask what it is precisely that is redeemed, and when we answer: the *whole* man, we have to consider all the factors that determine man's concrete existence. However, these do not consist merely in those two elements that define the inner nature of man — body and soul — but also in those elements of reality that come from the *outside,* without which there could be no human existence. These elements are often called the *existential* factors. Only when all these existential factors of human existence are included in Christ's redemption is the *entire* man saved.

There are three chief involvements that characterize the existence of bodily-spiritual man: his *involvement in the world, in community, and in history.*

Involvement in the World

Human life is not possible unless it encounters the world. Even the innermost life of the mind (knowledge, will, experience) draws its nourishment from the world in which man is rooted by reason of his body. Man cannot be perceived at all in his totality unless the world is also perceived along with him. Nor can man be redeemed as a total individual unless he is redeemed as a being rooted in or involved with the world. This is what Paul has in mind in his letter to the Romans when he writes that creation which was brought into the bondage of decay by man's sin, "waits with eager longing for the revealing of the sons of God" (cf. Rom. 8, 19-22). Through man, all of creation shares in redemption.

Involvement in Community

The human being does not stand alone in this world as an individual, but *in relation to society.* Certainly, as an individual person, man possesses his spiritual nature as his own, and possesses it uniquely, but he cannot develop nature except in community with other human beings. It is of course the mystery and the dignity of the human person that he is, in a very complete and unique way, a self-contained individual, so that he may know himself and make decisions in the freedom of his unique selfhood. But why is the human person given possession of himself in this way? Certainly not that he may make a shell of his selfhood and remain unfruitful, but rather that he may encounter other human beings. If the personal talents and capabilities of the human individual are to unfold, if he is to become completely *this* person (which at first he is only potentially, by the predisposition of his nature), then it is contact with others that must awaken his unique powers and stimulate them to growth. Thus involvement with human society is also an existential factor in determining man's life.

Involvement in History

A third important factor in the existence of man is his *presence in history*. In the life of the individual person there is not one moment in which he may be said to possess his existence completely. What he now is, he became as a result of his past, and this leads him to a future toward which he is reaching out. All of this, taken together, constitutes man. In fact there is even more: a human life, bearing the stamp of outside forces and internally shaped by the individual himself, is also determined by the history of the entire human community. The seemingly voluntary and solitary decisions made by the individual are codetermined by the forces of the human community, in which the forces of a long history have accumulated. We cannot deny that those decisions are free. However, even free and spontaneous decisions are made in relation to something. They do not arise in a vacuum; they have their roots in the soil of human society and its history. But history does not mean only the past. Since the past is to a great extent formed by the planned actions of human beings, and such actions were themselves planned with reference to a future, consequently even the future influences human life in the present moments. All of this means that man lives historically. This existential factor in human life must not be overlooked whenever we speak of the whole man. God did not overlook it in his intention to redeem the *whole* man.

2. REDEMPTION IS ADOPTION INTO A LIVING PARTNERSHIP WITH GOD

Having established that it is the whole man that is saved, we ask ourselves just how this salvation takes place. Only a look at Christ himself can answer this. Christ is not simply the author of our salvation; in him, as if in an original painting, God shows us what happens through salvation. It is well known to us that Christ obtained our redemption through his sacrifice on the cross, that he bought our freedom from the bondage of sin by means of that sacrifice. This of course tells us what act redeemed us, but it does not tell us what this act of redemption *involves* for us as its beneficiaries. This is shown to us in the God-Man, Jesus Christ. Salvation is nothing other than a sharing in the riches of Christ, a re-forming of human life in terms of Christ's divine humanity. This is why the Fathers of the Church tell us that the Son of God became the Son of Man in order that we, the children of men, might become the sons of God. Salvation is the participation of our human nature in the life of God as it was realized most perfectly and uniquely in the God-Man himself.

In the 4th century, when Apollinarius maintained that Christ did not possess a complete human nature, but that the second person of the Trinity took the place

of the human soul (or its higher functions) and appeared on earth in human form, the Fathers of the
Church rejected this erroneous teaching with the words:
"What has not been taken up (into the unity of life
with God), is likewise not redeemed." Salvation occurs
in the elevation of human nature, with everything that
belongs to it, into a living union with the Son of God.
This means first of all that Christ himself has taken on
a complete human nature. In Christ, the living union
between his individual human nature and the Son of
God is so perfect that in him there is no human person
as such, but rather only the divine person, who, in
Christ, is the bearer not only of a divine nature but also
of a human nature.

When the Son of God became man, he "came down
from heaven", as the Creed says. The infinite God
descended and humbled himself as a servant, "being
made like unto men" (Phil. 2, 6-8). At the same time,
this human nature was brought into a living union with
the Son of God. Naturally this did not happen in the
sense that Christ's adopted human nature had previously existed by itself and only later entered into a unity of
life with God. Christ's human nature was united with
the Son of God from the very first moment of its
existence.

All redemption shared by men is a participation in
this living union of Christ's humanity with the Son of
God. This participation is not the close and perfect
bond that exists in Christ himself, where both the
human and the divine nature belong to the one divine
person. However, it is nonetheless a genuine living partnership between man and God, brought about by God's
grace. Whatever in human actuality is not taken up
into this living unity with the second person of God
is not redeemed.

Redemption in the Church

We must now combine the two basic assertions examined above, namely, that the *whole* man is redeemed, and that this takes place through adoption into a *living partnership* with God. From this combination it is but a short step to the recognition that such redemption takes place in the Church. The Church is indeed the partnership of all men who, in their whole existential being, have been adopted into the living union with Christ in God. If God's plan for man's salvation is characterized by these two basic principles of the redemption of the *whole* man and his *life in community with Christ,* then the natural consequence is the founding of a Church in which the total man alone can be lifted up to that union of life with God.

A Church in the World

The whole man, we repeat, is adopted into a redeeming association with the God-Man. Since, however, man lives in this *visible* world, then that reality in which man is redeemed here and now must have a worldly form. It must be a part of the world so that it may serve as the ground in which man's religious, Christ-related life can also take root. A number of people are disturbed by the fact that the Church has a worldly structure, that she is an organization similar to many secular organizations, that she blesses the things of this world and even makes them the symbolic vessels of God's grace (the sacraments). Such persons forget that man is saved as a *total* being only as he exists in the midst of the world and stands in a *visible* community of life with God. Hence the Church, although not secularized, must be still a part of the world. In the Church the world encounters the life of God and is inwardly permeated and sanctified by him.

The Mystical Body

At the same time, man's communal nature, his relation to his fellowmen, must also be visibly brought into unity with Christ in order that this unity bear witness to the *redemption* of man-in-community. Where Christ's salvation has been imparted, the Christian community must bring to fruition not only man's natural and personal life but also his life of grace. That is the reason why Christ possessed not only a physical body, of which his disciples at the time could say: "We have seen with our eyes . . . and our hands have handled" (1 John 1, 1), but also extended that body, so to speak, to the *mystical body,* which is the community of the Church. In this mystical body the union of Christians with the Lord and with one another is so close that it is similar to the unity of the members of a physical body. It is *similar* but not the same, for in a natural organism the individual members have no independence. In the mystical body of the Church, on the other hand, the members are certainly brought into a living union with their divine-human head, but they do not thereby cease to be persons with the freedom of their own wills. They are indeed taken up into a life with Christ, but not without first giving their *personal assent* to this. Thus it is in the Church that the existential element in human life which we called a sense of community is realized with particular fullness and permeated by grace. When he enters into Christ's order of salvation, man need not put anything aside nor leave anything behind that defines his human existence in the natural realm. Through the community of the Church he shares in Christ's redemption, through adoption into the community of the Church which was established by Christ and which is constantly renewed around Christ as her center.

Salvation History

Finally, man is also redeemed in the Church in terms of his *historical being*. As a historical creature, man is lifted in the Church to a living union with God who entered our history. No one can deny that the Church actually makes her way through human history and does not live in a supra-historical realm of pure ideas. However, with the Church this path through history is not, as it is with other historical realities, simply a natural chain of historical events. In the Church, history becomes a *history of salvation*. Historicity, which is an existential factor defining man, is transformed in the Church into a redeeming factor of Christ's salvation. The Church passes through history from day to day, from year to year, and from century to century. To an extent she too is subject to the ebb and flow of historical circumstances. Nevertheless, the changes undergone by the Church through the centuries stand apart from those threatening factors that rob other historical realities of their permanence. Indeed, the Church's existence had its beginning in history, but it will not end in history. Rather, her existence will come to an end along *with* history. Only when there is no longer any history, when at "the consummation of the world" history will have been swallowed up by eternity, will the Church also cease to exist as a historical reality, so as to enter fully into the perfection of the Church Triumphant in eternity. Christ tells his Church that he will be with her always, "to the consummation of the world" (Matt. 28, 20). He makes himself the guarantee for the existence of the Church that will survive all the vicissitudes of history. Thus the Church signifies salvation for man in his historical dimension. His historical existence is affirmed. The belief of the Church in the apostolic succession, her emphasis on the apostolic tradition in doctrine and in life, show how very much she understands herself to be an historical reality. The Church, however, is the sole reality in which the human person is safe from the threat of history's impermanence, for in the Church God's eternal life is imparted to man.

The union of God with man, begun in Christ, has expanded in the Church into the dimensions of world, society and history. The Church is the extension of the divine will of salvation into all the levels of man's existence: the many facets of his being as an inhabitant of the world, the successive manifestations of his being in history, and the parallel aspects of his being in the human community. Thus God brings home to himself all the dimensions of human life, and into that realm which is "hidden with Christ in God" (Col. 3, 3).

WHY A UNIQUE CHURCH?

The Church will not continue to be an incomprehensible problem to the person who knows what the *total* human being is, and who knows that God has redeemed this total being in Christ. To some, however, it is less comprehensible why it has to be only *one*

Church, and just this particular one, in which that is
to happen.

Diversity, Not Contradiction

Among the numerous Churches existing today —
whether they be Roman Catholic, Lutheran or Re-
formed, Anglican, Greek Orthodox, or whatever —
would it not be possible to rediscover what the New
Testament tells us of the early Church? There also the
reference is to *Churches,* in the plural; one Church
greets another (e.g., Rom. 16; 1 Cor. 16, 19); there
is reference to the angels of the different Churches
(Apoc. 2-3). Is not the situation somewhat similar
with the great number of present-day Churches, with
their different names? Does not even the Catholic
Church admit to a great diversity of types and forms
within her own life, varying from culture to culture,
from nation to nation?

Variety not only can exist but *must* exist in the
Church if she is to remain a vital community. To many
of her forms of worship and prayer life the Church
today presents a different appearance than she did
centuries ago. Even the Uniate Church, i.e., the Eastern Churches united with Rome and thus belonging
to one Church, prays in a manner quite different from
that of the Western Church. Some forms of the religious life, and some liturgical forms, differ so much
between northern and southern regions that is is occasionally difficult to put up with their strangeness.
Also diverse is the manner of permeating human
thought with the truths of revelation. All of this, however, is diversity within the *unity* of the same Church.
When the New Testament speaks of different Churches,

it must be remembered that this word, *ecclesia,* designates both the entire worldwide Church as well as the individual local Churches or congregations. Thus it is not surprising that within the one large Church a local Church will send greetings to another, or that reference is made to the Church of Ephesus, or Smyrna, or Pergamum, etc.

On the other hand, when we consider the different organizations that today refer to themselves as *Church,* then we see not only variety composing a larger unity, but often the sharpest contradiction. This is not merely a consequence of the human rivalry and strained relations that can often exist within one Church, between one congregation and another, or between one person and another. On the contrary, what is proclaimed as truth in one of these Churches is rejected as error in another. Yet this sort of thing cannot be valid in the one and the same Church established by Christ, for the Church of Christ has nothing to proclaim but the truth revealed by *Christ.* For the fulfillment of this task the Church was promised the help of the Holy Spirit, who lives in her proclamation and preserves her in the truth (John 14, 16f.; 16, 13; 1 Tim. 3, 15). Thus in the case of the two Churches, when one proclaims the opposite of the other, there is only one explanation: only one of the two Churches can be the true Church established by Christ — unless, of course, we were resigned to the belief that the Church established by Christ still exists today. Such an attitude, however, could not rightly be interpreted as befitting human modesty, but rather would really amount to lack of faith in her trustworthiness and power of the Lord, who has promised to help his Church to the end of time.

For this reason the Church from the very beginning

has resisted nothing nearly so much as she has resisted *division*. How sharply Paul takes the Corinthians to task, when their congregation was on the point of splitting up into groups wanting to follow Peter, Paul and Apollos (1 Cor. 1, 10-13). When Jewish Christianity appeared to be threatened by the influx of Christians from among the Gentiles, the Church made every effort to preserve for the Gentile Christian communities a life of their own, without thereby endangering the unity of the Church (Acts 15). Paul sharply cautions his disciple, Timothy, against false doctrine (1 Tim. 4). In the time of the Church Fathers nothing was feared so much as a rending of the "seamless garment of Christ", to which the unity of the Church was likened.

Redemption as a Gift from Above

Where might this most profound justification be found for linking man's salvation not only to an ecclesiastical community but to this particular Church and this Church only? In order to understand the reason, we must consider that the Church knows she was founded by Christ in order that the entire work of God's salvation might take *visible form* in her. In this institution of salvation, it is to be made clear to mankind that *God* is at work in her history. Thus the clearly marked organization and firmly drawn institution of the Church are the visible manifestation of God's work of salvation among men. This manifestation of salvation through the Church means more than just a memory of a salvation effected at one particular time. This embodiment has the unique characteristic of also *transmitting* that salvation to the person who is a living member of it. If a person lives the life of the socially visible Church sincerely and honestly, then he has the guarantee that God's salvation and grace will be at work within him. For this reason the Church can be called a *sacrament* of salvation, since a sacrament is a symbolic manifestation of grace, at the same time conferring the grace it makes manifest.

Consequently, what should also become visible in the Church is just *how* God's salvation comes to man. The visible Church is to be a *sign* to men that God has made his home among them to effect their salvation. The very thing that strikes human beings as strange and even annoying — i.e., that they themselves cannot simply establish a Church whenever they please, but must follow the one and only Church that has come down to them through two thousand years — should really only show them that they are redeemed by the saving grace of God, and not by their own power. The notion, so frequently held today, that a Church can originate only through human decisions during the course of history, that is, "from the bottom up", is only a result of mistaken notions about redemption itself. Modern man likes to think of redemption only as self-redemption: redemption through philosophical thought, through scientific research, through techno-logical mastery of the world, through economic wisdom in the structuring of human society, or even through a self-forgetful plunge into the sea of pleasures. In these ways man seeks to liberate himself from the exigencies of the moment. Even if he concedes that redemption has come from God through Christ, he still prefers to explain the particular groupings that mankind has adopted around the redeeming Christ as ultimately being of human creation.

In truth, however, the Church is the visible representation of redemption through Christ. Since redemption is given as a gift *from above* and quite beyond human authorship, so also the Church as the manifest embodiment of this redemption must be constituted from above. The Church cannot be a democratic community, constantly originating from below, from the human level. The Church is *established* by the Lord. The only decision that can come from below is that of the individual who decides to let himself be caught up into the Church. Indeed, even this decision first comes from above: it is God's grace that must awaken it. To the extent that the individual freely accepts this grace or rejects it, this decision is of course also from below.

Therefore, it is not simply a matter of individual convenience to accept salvation within the framework of the Church or to remain outside of her as an individual: to choose according to one's taste whether one will be guided to salvation by this Church or that Church. Since salvation itself can come only from God, one must accept it in the form in which *God* offers it, namely, in Christ and his mystical body, which is the one Church established by him.

NO SALVATION OUTSIDE THE CHURCH?

This bond between the individual and the Church is so strong that according to the ancient conviction of the Church there can be no salvation outside the Church. Christ communicates the mission, which he himself received from the Father, to his apostles, on whom all authority of leadership in the Church is based (John 17, 18; 20, 21; Matt. 10, 40; Luke 10, 16). The Lord sends out his followers to make disciples of all nations and to baptize, that is, to receive them into the Church; to this mission he attaches a condition that makes human salvation dependent on the Church (Mark 16, 16). In his first letter to Timothy, Paul urges that prayers be said for *all* men, because God desires that all men be saved, and that this could happen only in the *unity of all* under the one God and the one mediator between God and men: Christ Jesus (1 Tim. 2, 1-5). This unity, however, according to Ephesians 4, 5 and the belief of the Church, can be achieved only through the one baptism and, therefore, in the one Church. Therefore, toward the close of our discussion another question faces us: "What of those who are outside the Church?" There are so many of them that the thought of their being eternally lost fills us with dread.

Meeting God in the Church

We must again clarify the basis for man's salvation only in the Church. The Church is the embodiment of God's will to save mankind. As the visible institution of salvation, the Church is the expression of God's concern for man. We must not forget one thing: if God's supernatural grace is really to save man, or make him *whole,* then it must nevertheless achieve this through *what man is by nature.* However, this does not happen simply by God's grace laying hold of a person without that person's knowledge. Christ's whole activity on earth showed that God really wants to *meet* man. He calls to man as a *person,* in order that man may voluntarily give access to God's approach to him. For this reason God *visibly* came to mankind in the person of Christ. For this reason he continues to give *visible* expression to his secret desire to save mankind, so that corporeal man can perceive him and take a stand with regard to him.

Even in the time before Christ, God made known his will to save mankind in the revelations of the prophets: "God, who at sundry times and in divers manners spoke in times past to the fathers by the prophets" (Heb. 1, 1). All this was only a preparation for the perfect way in which God would give expression to his saving will — by sending his own Son as his *Word* to mankind: "Last of all in these days he has spoken to us by his Son" (Heb. 1, 2.) However, this Word was to go on reverberating; it was not God's intention to have the visible expression of his divine will cease when Christ ascended into the invisible realms of heaven. He therefore established the Church as his mystical body; that visibility given to God's invisible will by Christ's earthly body was to be given continued expression in the Church. Just as a person does not hide the concern he has for someone else, but expresses it in actions and words, so God did not hide his concern for man's salvation, but gave it an expression that would be valid for all time through the founding of the Church.

From that point on, men must respond if they really desire to receive God's salvation. In what language and with what signs, however, shall man answer God? Surely in the language with which God began the conversation, with that sign in which God himself expressed his will to save man: namely, the Church. It is a commonplace of protocol that in a meeting it is the person of higher authority who determines the language and forms of expression to be used. It is also customary for the subordinate to wait until his superior extends his hand, in greeting or farewell, and then grasp the proffered hand. He meets his superior at a time

that is mutually beneficial after the superior has designated that time. Should we be surprised that things are
like this between God and man? God has designated
the meeting in which he turns toward us; he gives it
expression in the figure of Christ and his mystical body,
the Church. Therefore man can respond only in terms
of that uniquely valid form of expression, that is to say,
by meeting God as a member of the Church.

And Those Who Are Outside?

There are people who are inwardly ready to meet
God on his terms and who even give a certain human
expression of this readiness. They pray; they lead a
life of obedience to their conscience; perhaps they also
make sacrifices. However, they have not yet found the
one really *valid* way, laid down by God, for proper
encounter with him. Perhaps they will never find it
throughout their entire lives. Of course in the final
analysis it is necessary to *know* of this way and what
it means; in order to know, it is necessary first to have
heard. "How then are they to call upon him in whom
they have not believed? But how are they to believe
him [and to give this belief — we might add — the
right ecclesial expression] whom they have not heard?
And how are they to hear, if no one preaches?"
(Rom. 10, 14).

It would contradict the faith of the Church to say
that such people have no need for the Church, that
they would achieve salvation *without* the Church. They
too are designated for the Church and in actuality must
be in it. If they achieve the salvation of God, then it
is granted them for the sake of the Church: because
they live their lives in an attitude of conduct that *in*

and of itself can find appropriate expression only in the Church, and because this attitude would also lead them into the Church if they were aware of it. The Church is the necessary means for the salvation of man. No other way is given to man in his freedom of choice. This way of expressing the encounter was instituted for humanity by God himself through his own voluntary interposition. Man is bound to this expression. It can happen, however, that an individual is honestly ready to meet God on God's terms. This would in fact be a desire for the Church even without the individual's express knowledge of such readiness; yet his readiness has not found the expression instituted and stipulated by God. Should it not then be in God's power to accept even the first beginnings or the truncated vestiges of such expression for the genuine expression in its totality? The non-Catholic Christian is, after all, baptized and lives according to a number of forms of Catholic Church life. The individual who through no fault of his own was never baptized possesses, nonetheless, human nature and the forms of behavior before God which are a consequence of that nature. By reason of those forms, according to an ancient tradition, he still has a certain kinship and connection with the God-Man, the redeeming head of humanity. To make an analogy on the human level, all of us look with understanding on a child's first halting attempts at writing, or on the awkward expressions of a retarded person, when we know that they are doing the best they can and are not deliberately distorting the true forms of expression.

The principle that outside the Church there is no salvation still stands. The Church is the only *authentic* mode of encounter between God and man in Christ. However, in those who are outside the Church there can exist *incipient forms of the Church, or vestiges of churchliness,* by virtue of which they are disposed toward the true Church. If these people continue to be filled with the desire insofar as possible to express their encounter with God in the way he wants it expressed, then they live in an attitude of *openness to the Church,* through which, we may assume, they are adopted by grace into union with Christ and thus find their salvation.

STUDY-CLUB QUESTIONS

1. In what sense and from what point of view can the Church be seen as a problem?
2. The attempts to reconcile the idea of a Church having absolute claims with the demands of individual freedom seem to fall into three different categories. Can you describe each one? What is the difficulty with all three?
3. What is meant by the redemption of "the *whole* man"? Basically, how is redemption described?
4. Why is it important for us that Christ truly have a *complete* human nature? For the Church Fathers, what is the reason why the Son of God became the Son of Man?
5. How is the union of the members of the mystical body different from the unity of the members of a physical body?
6. In terms of his historicity, how is man redeemed in the Church?

7. Since variety must exist in the Church if she is to remain a vital community, would this not justify the presence today of the numerous organizations which refer to themselves as Churches? Explain.

8. In what sense can the Church be called a *sacrament* of salvation?

9. Under what forms does man tend to consider redemption as self-redemption? Does the Church agree with this?

10. On what basis do we say man finds his salvation *only in* the Church? How can the salvation of those *outside* the Church be achieved? Is there salvation *without* the Church? Explain.

IV
No Salvation
Outside the Church?

The Members of Christ's Body

INTRODUCTION

IN Part III, we explained why Christ made right conduct before God the business of the Church, and why he did not leave this responsibility to the private initiative of individuals or to independent groups who might form institutions for that purpose. The explanation ended with a brief discussion of the question concerning those who are *outside* the Church.

This question will occupy our special attention in Part IV. In an age of social pluralism it is not so very much the fact that there *is* a Church that causes the difficulty. If there is general approval of the combined efforts of many to achieve worthwhile goals in many areas of society, then such approval cannot reasonably exclude similar efforts in the field of religion. It would be inconsistent in a pluralistic society to be intolerant toward the Church as an instrument of religious fulfillment. If, however, it is not impossible for the Church to regard herself simply as one among many other religious institutions in society and she continues to claim to be the only legitimate embodiment of the community desired by God, then she is met by a lack of comprehension stemming from that same pluralistic attitude that is otherwise so commendably tolerant.

The teaching of the Church would certainly be more readily understood if she, though acting as an advocate of God, were at the same time in a position to concede to other religions and to other *Churches* that they, equally with her, were proclaiming the same laws of God.

It is part of the great burden of the Church that she must propose herself to mankind as both means and requirement for salvation. Even when her claim is not made ineptly, it is a difficult claim to state. However, her mission must not be left unproclaimed out of a false humility, for it is a mission given to the Church by Christ. It must therefore be seen, understood and fulfilled. It is hoped that the following considerations will contribute to that end. We must first recall to mind that the principle: "No salvation outside the Church," has been held by the Church from time immemorial. Therefore, despite the inevitable provocativeness of such a principle, the Church is obliged to proclaim it. It will then be our task to try to comprehend this statement correctly, so as to determine precisely what being "inside" or "outside" the Church means. Inasmuch as membership in the Church is necessary for salvation, the question of precisely who belongs to the Church is often and urgently asked today, both in Catholic theological circles and by those involved in inter-Christian dialogue.

THE CHURCH IS NECESSARY FOR SALVATION

It is not out of self-conceit that the Church feels

forced to insist that she is the unique path to salvation
— not merely one among many possibilities — mirror-
ing God's own exclusiveness. This unique role of the
Church stems from the heritage of an ancient belief,
based on the belief of the primitive Church as attested
in Scripture. Therefore, it is a belief that goes back to
Christ's revelation and his founding of the Church.

The Teaching of Tradition

The belief that there is no salvation outside the
Church finds its most emphatic and literal expression in
the writings of the 3rd-century Church Fathers. In
speaking of the necessity of the Church for salvation,
they even use the symbol of Noah's ark. Built according
to God's instructions, the ark offered rescue only to
those taken into it (Gen. 6, 13–8, 19). This image
speaks more impressively and categorically than any
verbal statement in words. Words, however, were also
used in that century to proclaim the necessity of the
Church for salvation. Origen, for instance, wrote in 250
A.D.: "Outside of this house no one can be saved."
The African bishop, Cyprian, puts it at that time a bit
more poetically: "No one can have God as father who
does not have the Church as mother."

When we consider that the writers of that day (who
were quite straightforward about the need for belonging to the Church) scarcely distinguished between guilt
and innocence in those outside the Church, then their
insistence on the point seems so severe as to be hardly
tolerable to us today. Consequently, the question of
precisely who is inside the Church and who is outside
becomes very important.

The 3rd-century formulation has biblical and apostolic roots. In the latter half of the 2nd century, Irenaeus, Bishop of Lyons, writes: "The truth that can be easily obtained from the Church must not be sought from others." Even at the turn of the 1st century, the martyred bishop, Ignatius of Antioch, writes to the Christians of Philadelphia: "Whoever follows anyone bringing about schism, that person will not inherit the kingdom of heaven."

The Testimony of Scripture

This awareness of the Church is not surprising. In Sacred Scripture, under the inspiration of the Holy Spirit, the claim of the primitive Church was already clear: the Church was the only path to salvation. The following statements clearly show the witness of the New Testament to the necessity of the Church for salvation.

The Symbolic References to the Nature of the Church

First, the various statements concerning the nature of the Church, statements clothed in imagery, convey at the same time the necessity of the Church for salvation. With its figurative expressions, Sacred Scripture opens up a wide field for faithful penetration of the depths of divine mysteries in the Church, mysteries which of course can be only incompletely captured in human language.

The following four images in particular tell us what the Church is. Arranged according to their relation to the three divine persons, these images first of all represent the Church as a *house* or as the *People of God*. By the word "God" the New Testament almost always means the first person of the Trinity, the Father. Here the Church is characterized as his possession. When the nature of the Church is mentioned in relation to Christ, her founder and redeemer, she is often called the *body* of Christ or the *bride* of Christ. It should be noted how these last two designations complement one another. As the body of Christ, the Church with her members forms a living union with him, a union that is super-natural and a mystery, but nevertheless real. Yet we must not exaggerate this union to the point of calling it an identity. In so doing we would forget that the Church and the individual persons belonging to her *confront* Christ, and stand opposite him, so to speak, just as two individual persons might stand facing each other. In this sense the Church can be aptly called the bride of the Lord, for she stands facing him, but in her love she is devoted to him and in turn is purchased and redeemed by him with the bridal price of salvation. Even in this confrontation, in this "opposition", the Church is united with Christ in a mysterious bond transcending any union on the human level. Christ and his Church "shall become one" (Eph. 5, 31).

This relationship of the Church to God the Father and her unity with Christ is realized through the Holy Spirit, who inwardly permeates the Church. That is why in the New Testament the Church is also called the *temple of the Holy Spirit*. When we consider that this temple of the Holy Spirit is the same Church that Paul also called the *body* of Christ, and that this temple is referred to as being built of "living stones" (1 Pet. 2, 5), then we understand why Leo XIII and Pius XII called the Holy Spirit the *soul* of the mystical body of Christ. He is the principle of the new supernatural life, alive in the Church, but in no way invalidating the natural life of man in the Church.

In our context these symbolic utterances on the Church are important because they all express her exclusiveness. There is no alternative to the Church as the People of God. In the New Testament the alternative to the People of God is not, for example, the people of the devil or the people of the world, but rather *"no people"* (1 Pet. 2, 10). One either belongs to the People of God, which is the Church, or one simply does not belong to a people having salvific significance in the eyes of God. The Church also has exclusiveness as the body and bride of Christ. Christ has only one bride, and she alone is united with him in one body. As the temple of the Holy Spirit, the Church is the sole pledge of the saving presence of the Holy Spirit. In the same way, the people of Israel in the Old Testament simply took for granted the uniqueness and exclusiveness of the temple of Jerusalem.

Baptism as Necessary for Salvation

A second way in which the New Testament clarifies that life in the Church is needed for salvation is in what is said about baptism. According to the New Testament, baptism is not simply a religious event existing for its own sake; rather through baptism the Church receives her members. On the day of Pentecost, when the power of the Holy Spirit swept away the disciples' fear, broke open the doors of their assembly hall and opened their locked and anxious hearts, the apostles began to preach. Those who listened gathered about the apostles. This entry into the community of the growing Church takes place not through mere personal decision on the part of individuals coming to the faith but, rather, by their being *baptized* and thus becoming members of the visible community of the Church. This metanoia or "turning" begins within the hearers of the Word in whom the Holy Spirit is working. However, this conversion finds its expression in baptism, through which the convert is visibly received into a visible community. It is in this community that the invisible life of grace with God has its visible sign and pledge. Precisely because baptism is the act through which the Church incorporates the faithful to herself — so that in her they belong to the one Lord and share in the life of the Spirit who fills them — the concepts of Lord, Spirit, body (the Church), faith and baptism belong together in the New Testament: "One body and one Spirit, even as you were called in one hope of your calling; one Lord, one faith, one baptism; one God and Father of all" (Eph. 4, 4–6).

According to the statement of the New Testament and the universal belief and conviction of the Church, baptism is the *necessary* means for attaining salvation. "Unless a man be born again of water and the Spirit, he cannot enter into the kingdom of God" (John 3, 5). Both these concepts, namely, that baptism is necessary for salvation and that through it we become members of the Church, are suggested in the first letter of Peter, who compares baptism to the *ark* that afforded the only means of rescue during the flood (1 Pet. 3, 20). The Church Fathers apply the same figure to the Church herself when they refer to her as the ark of salvation in the flood of iniquity. Since baptism brings us into the Church, it does not matter whether we compare baptism or the Church to the ark. The New Testament views faith as an inward decision, but a decision embodied in membership in the Church. The faithful are those who are in the Church. "He who believes and is baptized shall be saved, but he who does not believe shall be condemned" (Mark 16, 16). It is precisely this necessity of the Church for salvation which the New Testament is proclaiming when it says that baptism is necessary for salvation.

The Authority of the Apostles

A third reference to the same truth is made in the New Testament, when it associates salvation with the *apostles*. The apostles work in the name of Jesus and therefore must be heard and received by mankind (Luke 10, 16 and Matt. 10, 40). It is not possible to bypass the apostles and reach Christ. Not only is this put positively: "He who receives you receives me," almost as if there were no other means besides the apostles of finding the Lord, but the positive statement is completed by a negative one: "He who rejects you rejects me." Not even an angel from heaven has the authority to preach a Gospel contrary to the apostles' Gospel, or to proclaim a different salvation or a way of salvation differing from that proclaimed by the apostles (Gal. 1, 8). However, like baptism, the apostles do not exist for their own sake. They are the *foundation of the Church*. Peter is the rock on which the Church is built (Matt. 16, 16ff.). The apostles are the foundation (Eph. 2, 20; Apoc. 21, 14, 19), in whom Christ, the ultimate foundation of the Church (1 Cor. 3, 11), is visibly represented. If, therefore, one can build the salvation of his life only on the foundation of the apostles, and through them on the only foundation that is laid, namely Christ, then this salvation can be realized only in the Church.

Paul

Thus, it is not strange that we find in the letters of Saint Paul the conviction that the Church is necessary for salvation. Fellowship with God and with Christ, Paul tells us, exists only in the Church. It is in keeping with Saint Paul that we can say there is no salvation outside the Church.

The Teaching of the Magisterium

The teaching of the magisterium, therefore, adds nothing new or strange to the authentic teaching of the Church, when at different times throughout her history she insists that there is no salvation outside the Church. The magisterium, here as always, is advocating a doctrine that Christ and his apostles proclaimed. True, this principle was formulated in the medieval Church in ways that seem strange to us today. Boniface VIII writes very matter-of-factly in 1302: "We steadfastly believe and acknowledge in all simplicity that outside of [the Church] we will find neither salvation nor remission of our sins" (Denz. 468). The Decree of the Council of Florence in 1442, proclaiming to the Jacobites the necessity of salvation within the Church, seems harsh to us and difficult to understand: "The holy Roman Church believes, professes and preaches that no one remaining outside the Catholic Church, not just pagans, but also Jews or heretics or schismatics, can become partakers of eternal life; but they will go to the 'everlasting fire which was prepared for the devil and his angels' (Matt. 25, 41), unless before the end of life they are joined to the Church . . . And no one can be saved, no matter how much alms he has given, even if he sheds his blood for the name of Christ, unless he remains in the bosom and the unity of the Catholic Church" (Denz. 714). It is somewhat easier to understand this late medieval text if we realize that what is always meant in such documents is a *culpable* separation from the Church, and that the question of whether one can be outside the Church and also *without* culpability is not considered here.

In more recent times the magisterial texts, whenever they speak of the necessity of the Church for salvation, make a much clearer distinction between culpable and inculpable separation from the Church. Thus in 1854 Pius IX emphasized very strongly: "It must, of course, be held as a matter of faith that outside the apostolic Roman Church no one can be saved, that the Church is the only ark of salvation, and that whoever does not enter it will perish in the flood." However, he adds no less forcibly: "On the other hand, it must likewise be held as certain that those who are affected by ignorance of the true religion, if it is invincible ignorance, are not subject to any guilt in this matter before the eyes of the Lord" (Denz. 1647).

Therefore, if we are to interpret correctly the necessity of belonging to the Church in order to attain salvation, we must include the question of personal responsibility, which determines whether or not people belong to the Church. In 1949 in a letter to Archbishop Cushing of Boston, the Holy Office declared, in order to correct an all too narrow interpretation by an American priest (Leonard Feeney) of the principle, "no salvation outside the Church": "Among those principles which the Church has always proclaimed and will never cease to proclaim is also that infallible article of faith which teaches us that there is no salvation outside the Church. This dogma however is to be understood in

the sense in which the Church herself understands it
. . . In his infinite mercy God willed that the effects of
those necessary means of salvation, which are directed
toward the final goal only through divine ordinance but
not from any inner necessity, can also be attained even
if these means are applied only in 'wish' (*voto*) and in
'desire' (*desiderio*) . . . In order for anyone to achieve
eternal salvation it is not always required that he be an
actual member of the Church; but it is necessary at least
that he follow the Church in wish and in desire. It does
not always have to be an express wish, as it is among
the candidates for baptism. If the individual is in a state
of invincible ignorance, God also accepts a wish for
inclusion, which is so called because it is contained in
that attitude of soul in which the individual wants to
have his will conform to the will of God" (Denz. 3866-
3870).

THE CHURCH AND SALVATION

What we have up to now gathered from the *sources*
of the Church's faith we must now seek to understand
from the Church's inner meaning. Since we, as persons
in the faith, have been touched by God and called to
decision, the question of that meaning must be examined. Belief must become a listening to God's Word,
a listening that seeks to penetrate the depths of what is
heard, in the conviction that God wants something of
us. In these depths, however, lies the *reason* for the
belief. If we want to understand *why* the Lord created
the Church as an institution necessary for salvation,
then we must seek to understand how salvation and the
Church are related to one another. Two questions have
to be answered: (1) *What is this salvation,* whose at-

tainment requires membership in the Church? (2) How does *life* in the Church *relate* to this *salvation?*

What Is This Salvation?

The German word *Heil* (salvation) has the fundamental meaning of *wholeness* or *entirety*. However in the actual order of salvation that we are discussing, this wholeness cannot be explained in a purely positive way, as though it were an undisputed reality having an independent existence. This wholeness or salvation, in the context of the Christian faith, means the *restoration* of a wholeness that has been lost. It is a *healing* of a disability, an overcoming of a deficiency. The absolute original condition of human existence was certainly a wholeness, from which the human race fell because of the disastrous disobedience of its ancestor and original head. Since then there has been disorder in the life of the individual person — the original fault from which he must first be rescued or *healed* by immersion into the mystery of the death and resurrection of the Savior in baptism. This disorder at the start of the history of the human individual and of the history of mankind is not suffering and death, but sin as a separation from God in whose disfavor man now stands. The suffering and inescapable death, which according to God's original will were to have been withheld by the intervention of grace, came upon mankind as a consequence of sin and became the visible evidence of that invisible disaster of separation from God that could not be directly experienced. The suffering we experience in the present order of things is a *sign* of the calamity of sin.

Salvation means rescue from this calamity. Salvation is not earthly well-being, although the two have some-

thing in common. When Old Testament man, in the
light of the then incomplete divine revelation, thought
he saw a direct demonstration of God's favor in a happy
earthly life, he was not entirely mistaken. Of course this
view was considerably corrected by the revelation fulfilled in Christ. He who shares in God's salvation may
also hope for earthly well-being and see in this a sign,
a foretaste, a presentiment of the gift of salvation itself. What *really* matters, however, is not earthly well-
being, but rather *happiness* with God, which on earth
begins to be realized in *grace*. The happiness of heaven
consists essentially in divine blessedness due to God's
communication of himself to man. Thus grace, as the
beginning of salvation on earth, is God himself insofar
as he intimately communes with man and from this
indwelling causes man to grow toward a new reality in
a genuine though incomplete participation in the union
of human nature with God, as it occurred when God
became man.

We can equate this salvation with what Sacred Scripture calls the sovereignty of God; thereby, its relation
to the Church is suggested. We do better to translate
the Greek *basileia tou Theou* as "sovereignty of God"
rather than "kingdom of God". The word "kingdom"
evokes the image of a complete and clearly defined ter-
ritory, while in Sacred Scripture the point is the sovereignty of God, working to the extent that it becomes
operative in man and constituting man's salvation. For
this sovereignty of God, and thus this salvation, to be
realized, it must be operative on *both* sides. *God* has to
give of himself to man in grace, permeate man's being,
and (as the Eastern Fathers were fond of putting it)
"divinize" him. However *man* must *acknowledge* this
loving sovereignty of God; he must make God's will
the law of his life and obey it. Certainly it is not man

who builds the kingdom and dominion of God, but God himself. If a person does not receive God and acknowledge that he is Lord, then God's sovereignty and salvation are not accomplished in *that* person.

The Relation between Church and Salvation

Christians believe that the Church is here to serve in accomplishing man's salvation. However, how is this to be done? There are various answers. The principle from which we began — no salvation outside the Church — implies that salvation is in the Church. It is therefore necessary to clarify what salvation *in* the Church means. Three views of the relationship between Church and salvation are frequently encountered. Two of these are erroneous extremes; the truth lies somewhere between them.

Mistaken Conceptions

One extreme makes the matter too simple by merely *equating* salvation with the Church. In this view, the kingdom or sovereignty of God is precisely the Church. Were this view correct, then the doctrine of the necessity of the Church for salvation would be easily explained. It is clear that we must have salvation to attain heaven, for the happiness of heaven *is* salvation. So if the Church and salvation simply coincided, then the necessity of the Church for salvation would be simply the logical conclusion, even a tautology.

This view, however, is too simple and contradicts the following facts. There are also sinners in the Church, people who have lost salvation by turning against God.

As long as they are alive on earth, this loss is not final, but in their state of unrepented sin they are excluded from *salvation*. Nevertheless they remain members of the *Church*. One does not cease to belong to the Church by reason of sin alone, even though this is sin against the Church. If this is so, then the Church cannot be simply identical with salvation. A reverse observation will confirm the same thing. There are people who through no fault of their own are outside the visible Church, but concerning whom we may reasonably hope that they share in salvation, in divine grace. The previously quoted letter of the Holy Office to the Archbishop of Boston stated that expressly. The Church and Church membership cannot therefore be simply identical with salvation and the attainment of salvation. To equate them would *exaggerate* the relation between Church and salvation.

The *other extreme* is just as mistaken. Here the relation of the Church to salvation is viewed too superficially. Salvation seems to be an event taking place privately between God and the individual person. According to this view, the Church need only see to it that people prepare themselves for God and his grace. She merely makes the arrangements, so to speak, and supplies officials under whose influence people are supposed to render themselves receptive to the gift of God's grace. This takes place through teaching and admonition, just as it might in any school. Here the Church plays the role of a mother bringing her child to the dentist; by means of threats and cajolery she persuades the child to enter the waiting room, and perhaps even accompanies him to the treatment room. Perhaps she even goes so far as to help the dentist by opening the child's mouth. However, the actual dental work is a matter between the child and the doctor alone.

This view of the role of the Church in salvation is encountered frequently enough. It is, however, inadequate and wrong. If it were the task of the Church only to make arrangements and prepare mankind in this way, her necessity for salvation would be at most a very relative thing, restricted to children and the *immature,* who need authoritative leadership and guidance for their way to God. In this view, anyone sufficiently mature, alert and close to God could easily dispense with the mediation of the Church. There could even be a tendency for the Church to make herself unnecessary for the individual as soon as possible, just as in the natural realm the good educator must consider himself as having succeeded when his pupil reaches that degree of maturity which permits him to face life without a tutor. The doctrine of the absolute and irreplaceable necessity of the Church for salvation shows this superficial interpretation of that relationship to be inadequate.

Between the Extremes

Here also the truth lies between the two extremes. An identity of Church and salvation would be too much, while a merely maternal and tutorial Church, with no part in completing the process of salvation, would be too little. The true relationship contains some elements of both positions. Salvation and the Church are two realities, but they belong together in a living unity. They are so very much a living two-in-oneness that, while we must not make them identical, we must not seek the kingdom of God outside of the Church nor bypass the Church in our search for salvation.

We are already familiar with this relationship from the *sacraments.* The Church, the visible, social Church established by Christ, is also a sacramental reality. Just as individual sacramental acts are a symbol and pledge of the event or growth of salvation in mankind, so also the visible Church is a sacrament for those embodied in her; she is a symbol and pledge of salvation. A sacrament is both a sign and a cause or pledge of salvation. This cause, however, operates in a unique way: it is not like a hammer used for driving a nail. Neither the nail nor the board into which it is driven can have the freedom to decide whether nailing will take place or not. However, God in his grace and the one to whom that grace is given through the sacraments are *personal* realities. The grace is *God,* who gives himself to the individual and *shares* with him his divine life. *Man receives* this grace through the sacrament as an *instrument,* not as a piece of wood receives the nail driven into it, but rather as a *person,* who must stand before the God of grace and decide whether he is willing to accept that grace.

For this to happen, however, the spiritual reality of God must acquire some kind of physical form. Man can make a decision with regard to something only if it first externally confronts him, and then becomes interiorized through the free "Yes" of his decision. A spiritual reality must first knock at the door of our senses, so to speak, to gain entry to the inner nature of our person. That is why, after he had already become embodied in Jesus Christ in the incarnation, the Lord clothed his grace in the symbols of the sacraments. Seeing these signs, man can and should decide whether he will receive them and, in them, the grace of God. Yet the sacraments represent grace only figuratively; they also bear within them, through Christ's institution, the power of imparting grace to man if he freely decides to open himself up.

The Church is in a similar situation. She is the symbol of salvation. The community of the Church is the representation, the image, the sign, of that community of life with God in which salvation consists. She is a sacramental symbol. If man enters into this symbol and lives the life of the Church in personal decision, then a pledge is given to him that he is really receiving the salvation represented and symbolized by the Church.

What is the significance of all this? Belonging to the visible Church is simply not the same thing as the grace or the salvation symbolized and promised by her. One is the symbol and the other is what is symbolized. Both things can even actually be separated from one another in the individual person, if a member of the visible Church has lost salvation and grace through sin; or, conversely, if an individual through no fault of his own is not a member of the visible Church, yet exists in a state of grace. These two realities, however, are not independent of one another; by virtue of God's ordinance they are inwardly interlinked. Membership in the visible Church does not fulfill its purpose if the individual in his sin rejects the grace that should be represented in and mediated by the Church. The grace of salvation is so closely bound up with membership in the Church that no man at his own discretion would be able to take or leave the Church: to become a part of her or seek the way to God by himself.

Because of this, it is possible for man to receive salvation in a way that harmonizes with his human and personal nature. He should receive grace *as a human being*. In receiving grace his human nature is to be fulfilled. They are mistaken who think it unworthy for a living human being, endowed with a mind, to receive the grace of God through the visible mediation of the Church and not directly from God himself. In reality, man should receive God's grace in an affirmative response to God's personal call to him. Certainly God, as absolute spirit, would be capable of profoundly stirring man without the mediation of man's senses. However, it would not be possible then for man to say yes or no. That is why God first stands at the door of the human senses and knocks: so that man may decide whether he will permit him to enter his inner existence. Man must give expression to this acceptance of, and surrender to, God in a form that will include in his encounter with God all the dimensions in which human existence is realized. It is as a *spirit in a body,* as an *individual in society,* as a *person* rooted *in the world* and as a *human being* living here and now, with his origins *in history* and entering into history, that man must give expression to his encounter with God.

Thus the form in which the human-divine encounter is expressed is determined to a great extent by human nature. Its real form and definition, however, must come from God. Whenever two partners of unequal position meet and deal with one another, it is the superior who determines the language and mode of expression. In the meeting between God and man, especially in the supernatural order conferred on man by grace, it is for God to determine the expression this salvific encounter is to take.

This is what we mean when we say that the Church was *established* by Jesus Christ. In his life with the disciples, the God-Man, through his sacrificial death on the cross and the event of Pentecost, founded the Church in her essential corporeal structure and filled her with the divine principle of life, the Holy Spirit. The Church contains all the dimensions covered in human existence: *personal inwardness,* since the life in the Church demands a personal decision; the human *body,* since the Church is perceived and lives through the medium of the senses; the relationship to *society,* since the Church is established as a social reality; roots in the *world,* since the Church brings a part of the world to be permeated by God; and existence in *history,* since the Church, even though established by Christ once and for all, nevertheless develops and lives historically. On Pentecost God gave assurance that the Church signifies the presence of his salvation among men, and that she is the expression of his will for the salvation of mankind. This obliges man to make that same Church the expression of his surrender to God. Whoever wishes to meet God in salvation must therefore be in the Church. Whoever through his own fault would remain outside her would be excluded from the gift of God's grace.

Hence we must now ask: "Who then is in the Church, and more specifically, in her in such a way that his membership is a pledge of the gift of God's grace?"

WHO IS IN THE CHURCH?

This question will be treated in three subsections. First we will show what being in the Church in the *full sense* means in terms of external and internal factors. Then we will show how full Church membership can be *diminished* from the standpoint of those factors. Finally, we will discuss the question of *who is outside,* in relation to the principle of "no salvation outside the Church".

Meaningful Membership in the Church

To begin with, membership in the Church is determined by external elements. Since the Church is a sacramental symbol and a pledge of salvation, she and membership in her must be seen as symbol and pledge. This does not exclude the view that the inner reality of salvation is mediated sacramentally by the Church. However, as we have already seen, the Church is not the same thing as salvation, but rather its *symbol* and *pledge*. Therefore when we speak of belonging to the Church, we must first direct our intention to the external factors perceivable by the senses.

Membership in the Visible Church

According to the Catholic faith, there is a threefold bond for complete membership in the Church.

The first bond is the *symbolic* bond between man and the Church. Here "symbolic" means the confession of faith that affirms the truth revealed by Christ and proclaimed by the Church under the guidance of the Holy Spirit.

The second bond is the *sacramental* bond, established by reception into the Church through the sacrament of *baptism*. Since baptism has a bearing on all the other sacraments, especially the eucharist, and since baptism, as indissoluble, enables the baptized individual to participate fully in those other sacraments, they also belong to this sacramental bond. Here the eucharist plays a special role because it forms the center of life in the Church and embodies the Church in the fullest and most explicit way. The eucharist is the essential sacrament of Church unity.

The third bond is the *hierarchical* one, in which the believer acknowledges the pastoral function that Christ established in his Church as a vicarious representation

of his own function as shepherd. This is the hierarchy
of bishops, with the pope as the uniting head of the
college of bishops and of the entire Church. This hierarchy is not merely a kind of managerial power, which
of course in one form or another exists also in non-
Catholic Christian communities. Rather, it guarantees
the unity of the Church only where it has been handed
down from generation to generation in an *unbroken
line* from the apostles by the laying on of hands and by
commission. This hierarchical factor does not simply
parallel the symbolic and sacramental bonds of unity
in the Church; it permeates them both and gives them
meaning. The faith that must be affirmed in the confession of faith is proclaimed, with the guidance of the
Spirit of God, by the hierarchy established by Christ.
The administration of the sacraments must be directed
by the pastoral authority of the ecclesiastical hierarchy,
if participation in these sacraments is to confer complete membership in the Church.

The Inner Aspect of This Membership

This threefold bond, which binds the individual person to the visible Church community, is first of all an
external reality; it involves the confession of faith and
the reception of the sacramental symbols and social
submission to the hierarchical order. It is clear, however, that these externals must not exist for their own
sake. A sign must be connected with what it signifies.
When we ask who belongs to the Church in the full
sense of the word, the three forms of relationship mentioned above must also be considered from their inner
aspect.

A person may belong to the Church as an external
reality even if he confesses the faith but does not in-

wardly affirm it; if he receives the sacrament without
being inwardly prepared; if he outwardly obeys the
hierarchy of the Church, but inwardly follows his own
will. It is clear that the very heart is missing from this
kind of membership in the Church, for the inner meaning of the outward belonging is not fulfilled. An individual belongs to the Church in the full sense of the
word if, as a member of the Church, the symbol of
salvation, he also possesses the *grace* symbolized by the
Church; only in this way does he rightly fulfill the
inner meaning of his membership. Consequently, only
that person belongs to the Church in the fullest sense
who also stands in God's grace and has not forfeited
this grace through sin.

Incomplete Membership in the Church

If complete membership in the Church must com-
prise both outer sign and the inner grace signified by
that sign, then it is possible for Church membership
to become incomplete in either of those two areas. It
becomes incomplete when any of the three previously
mentioned "bonds" constituting outward and visible
Church membership are missing. Membership can also
become defective when, though it satisfies all outward
requirements, it no longer fulfills its inner meaning;
when it is no longer ratified by the grace that it is
supposed to signify and communicate to man. Membership in the Church is deprived of meaning and
impaired in its genuine realization, whenever any member is separated through sin from God, whose grace
ought to be signified and communicated by membership in the Church.

Thus, if an individual is validly baptized but belongs

to a Christian denomination that does not profess the entire content of the faith taught by the Church in the name of Christ, or does not celebrate all of the remaining sacraments besides baptism, or does not acknowledge the episcopal and papal hierarchy established by Christ, then certainly a real bond still exists between that individual and the Church. His baptism is a reality that he himself cannot lose and that the Church cannot ignore. Certain elements essential to *full* membership in the Church, however, are lacking. Since he does not choose his incomplete status by reason of personal knowledge and responsibility, such an individual cannot be called a member of the Church in the complete sense even though he is in possession of God's *grace*. God's grace, even though God has bound it to the Church, can also come to the person who belongs to the Church only partially, but through no fault of his own. For example, the separated Christians of the Eastern Church profess almost the entire faith in common with us, and they celebrate the seven sacraments with us. They even recognize a valid episcopal hierarchy handed down by apostolic succession, but they deny the primacy of the pope. They embody very many elements in common with the Church, but they do not have full membership in the Church. The denominations stemming from the Reformation share considerably less in common with the Church. In many points of faith they do not profess the same things we do. Of the sacraments, they still have only baptism. The eucharist is celebrated in Protestantism, but there are no priests empowered through sacramental consecration; their clerical function no longer has the essential mark of apostolic succession. However, even in these denominations there exist real bonds with the Church, and even in their incompleteness they are moving through these defects toward fulfillment and integration into full membership in the Church.

In addition, the person in serious sin, having gone against God's will and sovereignty and thereby suffered the loss of God's grace, lacks much that ought not to be lacking in a vital membership in the Church. He may be in the Church to the extent that she is a *sign* of salvation. He has lost, however, that living communion with God in grace symbolized by union with the Church and which is its meaning and content. He has deprived his membership in the Church of its truth. Even outward membership in the Church is no longer without defect in the case of such a person, for whoever has lost inward grace through sin can no longer fully enter into the sacramental bond with the Church. This bond does not consist merely in reception into the Church through baptism. Baptism enables the individual to participate in the most central sacramental bond of the Church, namely the eucharist. In it he receives the sacrificial body of Christ, present in the sacrament, in order to share in the life of the mystical body of Christ which is the Church. Paul impressively describes this union of the eucharistic and mystical body of Christ when he says: "The bread that we break, is it not the partaking of the body of the Lord?" (1 Cor. 10, 16). That body, whose communion the eucharist signifies and effects, is according to Paul the ecclesiastical body of the Lord; a share in the life of that body is signified and communicated by participation in the eucharistic body of Christ. Therefore, that person whom sin has cut off from the sacramental participation in the eucharist is no longer an unbroken link in the membership of the Church.

We now face the most important question in our

discussion: "Who then is outside the Church in such a way that he is deprived of salvation?"

WHO IS OUTSIDE THE CHURCH?

We have established that one cannot simply be "in" or "out" of the Church, but that even an individual who is not a member of the Church in the full sense nevertheless has a real relationship to the Church in that he is partially a member. Therefore, we must not expect a hasty "either-or" answer to the question of who is outside the Church. We must ask our question in stages: "Who is outside the Church in such a way that this exclusion would mean a loss of *salvation?*" Then we must ask: "Is it perhaps possible for a person to be outside the visible Church and yet be able to share in the salvation which, properly speaking, can be obtained only inside the Church?"

Outside the Church and Outside Salvation

We must not weaken the Church's traditional teaching concerning membership in her as a requisite for salvation in such a way that we can no longer reckon with the possibility that someone who is outside the Church may be deprived of salvation. Of course there are individuals who are not fully in the Church, but who nevertheless share in salvation and are in God's grace. This kind of "being outside the Church" is, however, not the same as that exclusion intended by the ancient principle of "no salvation outside the Church". When do we have an exclusion admitting of no salvation?

We have it when, first of all, the individual does not realize any of the previously mentioned relationships to the Church — confession of the faith proclaimed by the Church, the bond of the sacraments, the acknowledgment of the hierarchy established by Christ. A loss of salvation results from the lack of this threefold tie to the Church if the lack is the *personal fault* of the individual, i.e., an expression of his erroneous decision, freely made.

By this we do not mean only that culpable decision that is made directly against a relationship with the Church herself. Culpable loss of Church membership and, with it, a loss of salvation can also be caused by the guilt that makes an individual, in his basic attitude and disposition, no longer open to the call of the God who wants to lead this individual to the Church or again make him a vital member of her. Then, too, one who is fully a member of the visible Church can, nevertheless, through a life set against God, fall into an attitude so opposed to the meaning of membership in the Church that he can no longer detect nor even believe in that meaning; he therefore separates himself from the Church. This would also be *culpable* separation from the Church. It may be that the act of this separation itself might take place without full insight and freedom, and would therefore not be a sin in any *immediate* sense. However, the sin would exist *previously,* in a life lived in sinful contradiction to the meaning of the Church and turning separation from her into an exclusion that rejects salvation.

This, then, is the situation of the individual who is outside the Church in such a way as to be cut off from salvation. The external ties to the visible Church are missing in such a way that their absence is the consequence and sign of an inner, sinful separation from

God. Is there also a state of being outside the Church which, of course, would not imply full participation in the Church, but would not mean the loss of salvation due to separation?

Not Fully in the Church Yet within Salvation

The truth remains: a person clearly not in the visible Church, in no way tied to her by an objective bond based on his will and desire, and at the same time not even subjectively bound to her by a direction or life that would at least include a desire for the Church willed by God — such a person is outside of salvation. Outside of the Church, then, there is no salvation. However, this "outside the Church" is not quite so simple to determine as the words may seem to indicate.

The question might be asked: "What possible purpose could be served by looking for a more precise sense of 'outside the Church', when it seems to be sufficient for salvation not to be outside in every respect?" It is nevertheless important to be more precise here. It is of course true that it is also possible to be in the Church in an *extended sense*. In other words, a person not fully in the Church through no fault of his own, because of no better knowledge, nevertheless is related to the Church in such a way that he may secure salvation by reason of certain partial realities of Church membership that he still embodies. This condition, however, is incomplete and presses toward completion by virtue of an inward dynamic stemming from the act of Christ's establishment. Therefore, whenever the visible tie with the Church is only incompletely realized because of invincible error and therefore inculpability of the person involved, nevertheless, even though such a person can obtain God's grace through this partial relationship, it is not left up to the person and to the Church to be content with this state of affairs. Whatever incompletely realizes the institution of the Lord must, insofar as possible, be made whole. Even though these incomplete elements may be sufficient for the salvation of the individual person, since he is not responsible for their deficiency, their faulty character must nevertheless be made known. The Church herself, as the establishment of Christ, has the responsibility for making these defects known. Individuals, or even groups of individuals, may without personal guilt fall short of this establishment. This, however, does not give the Church any right to negligence in proclaiming what is needed for full existence in the Church.

How can an individual be not fully in the visible Church and yet share in the salvation of God's grace? Such a case is characterized by two factors. On the one hand, this person does not embody all of the elements connected with the visible, social Church established by Christ. Perhaps for want of better knowledge he does not profess all of the truths of faith of the Church, or he lives in a Christian denomination that does not celebrate all seven sacraments, or, because he does not know of its establishment by God, he is not subject to the hierarchy of the pope and the bishops. On the other hand, he nevertheless has that will, that attitude of submission to God, which could potentially be expressed in the membership of the true Church desired by the Lord, but whose full expression this person has, through no fault of his own, not yet found. Should not God in this case be content with a part of that faulty expression which this person has achieved and is carrying out in good faith?

The Church bids us hope that such a person possesses salvation. He is open to God's sovereignty within him to the extent that he would like to do God's will, expressed in the establishment of the Church as an embodiment of his kingdom. This person does not know that God's will requires membership in the Catholic Church under the successor of Peter. Since he does not know this, he does not bear responsibility for it. If he knew it, then he would follow this will of God. Such readiness, even though not explicit, is already an obedience to this will. Those partial elements of his relationship to the Church that he does realize bind him effectively, despite their incompleteness, to the real and only true Church of Christ.

The situation, however, is more difficult for a person who is not even baptized and does not realize any of the elements of the Church established by Christ, even though this may stem from lack of better knowledge. Even so, if he is receptive to God's will and lets his life be guided by it, we can see in his human nature, which relates him to the incarnate Son of God, at least a start in the direction of the Church. Such a beginning makes salvation possible if through no fault of his own this person should come no closer to membership in the Church.

For all who stand in an incomplete relationship to the Church, the salvation they achieve is none other than the salvation of those in the Church. There is no other salvation than that which the Church communicates. Those who belong only incompletely to the Church, or who are merely disposed toward her, possess salvation, when they do possess it, as a result of their tie with the Church, however incomplete that may be. The one and only Church, desired and established by Christ, is always the symbol and pledge of salvation for all mankind, including those who are not entirely within her fold because their knowledge is incomplete.

STUDY-CLUB QUESTIONS

1. What claim of the Church is difficult for a pluralistic society to accept? Why?

2. Give some examples, from early writings of Church
   Fathers, of the conviction that there is no salvation outside the Church. What are some of the
   ancient images or symbols of the Church and
   what do they all attempt to convey?

3. What is the significance of the New Testament
   assertion that baptism is necessary for salvation?
   Explain.

4. What relationship does the authority given the
   apostles have to this discussion of the Church as
   necessary for salvation?

5. In recent magisterial texts on the necessity of the
   Church for salvation, what distinction is stressed?

6. What does salvation mean? What is the relationship between salvation and the Church? How can
   you describe the two erroneous extremes?

7. In what sense is the Church a "sacrament"?
   Explain.

8. Why must man "make the Church the expression of his surrender to God"?

9. Describe the threefold bond that gives rise to full membership in the Church.

10. What is the inner meaning of membership in the Church? How can an individual be outside the Church in such a way as to be cut off from salvation? How can an individual share in salvation and yet not be fully in the visible Church?

V
Criticism of the Church

A Right and Its Limits

INTRODUCTION

THAT the Church is open to criticism is regarded by most people (at least judging from their practice of it) as self-evident. It is just as self-evident to others that criticism of the Church must be rejected; this is especially the case when the minority is shocked by criticism and reacts in a kind of instinct of self-preservation. It is precisely that assumption, on both sides, of the self-evident certainty of their position that makes us suspect that neither side is coming very close to the full truth involved. The critics' delight is sometimes really a malicious pleasure in the failure of a great institution that has evoked a reluctant admiration. The defensive attitude of those repelled by the criticism, even though fortified with arguments based on the nature of the Church, often serves as a kind of armor beneath which the criticized seek to hide their uncertainty.

May the Church be criticized or not? The Catholic view of the Church emphasizes something that renders

her immediately subject to criticism — i.e., the assertion that she was established as a visible Church by
Jesus Christ. Her visibility means that people can point
at her. She must also recognize that she is "pointed at"
with all the shades of meaning implied by that expression. If the Church is to be counted as a visible reality
within the structure of human society, then she not only
cannot avoid being pointed at (perhaps even mali-
ciously), but she must also accept this as an occasion
for candid self-examination.

There is, however, a unique aspect to this visibility
of the Church. Our Protestant brothers are accustomed
to remind us of the words of Bellarmine, so scandalous
to them, in which he compares the visibility of the
Church to the visibility of the kingdom of Naples. Yet
a comparison, as we all know, is not the same thing
as an equation.

With his comparison Bellarmine no more makes
the Church equivalent to a temporal State than does
the scriptural saying that Christ became like us "in
all things except sin" (Heb. 4, 15) erase the difference
between us and the incarnate God.

It is, therefore, not merely a defensive reaction stemming from human uncertainty but, due to the very
nature of the case, that criticism of the Church is
subject to some reservations and limitations. The right
to criticize the Church stems from faith in the mystery
of a Church in which God's salvation not only works
within a visible human community, but is also subject
to human and even sinful shortcomings. Faith in the
Church will not deny criticism of the Church; the right
to criticize is ultimately based on the self-denial of the
Lord himself, who took the form of a servant (Phil.
2, 7) and thus exposed and continues to expose himself
to criticism in his Church, whose visible form must be

realized by sinful human beings. However, a certain unique ambivalence about the Church makes an unqualified acceptance of criticism as impossible as a simple refusal to criticize. Scriptural statements about the Church sometimes carry two meanings. One meaning will assign the Church to the realm of human experience and thus also to human criticism, while the other meaning puts the Church so close to the Lord that critical attack, although not rendered impossible, becomes difficult, and we must be careful not to naturalize and oversimplify. The Church is a "people", but a people "of God"; she is a "body", but in a mysterious way the body "of Christ"; she is a "bride", but the bride "of the Lord"; she is a structure, a "house", or "temple", but one inhabited by the Spirit of God. Criticism of the Church must also respect this ambivalence, if it is to fulfill its task.

The possibility for a criticism of the Church is a consequence of the Church's faith in her own visible character. This will be taken up in the first part of our discussion. Criticism of the Church, however, has to be aware of the difficulty confronting it. This difficulty stems mainly from the vitality of the Church in human society and history; this difficulty becomes an appeal to conscience because of the sacred nature of the Church. More about this, however, in the second part of our discussion.

VISIBILITY IMPLIES CRITICISM

If the Church insists so strongly on her visible nature as established by Christ, she then subjects herself to a possible, justifiable, and even necessary criticism.

What precisely do we mean by the visible Church?
Christ did not build his Church chiefly as a house in
which people would enter and live as though they were
mere residents instead of really *being* this Church or
her members. All figures of speech are valid only from
certain definite points of view. This also is true for the
figure of the Church as a house or, to use a popular
early comparison, as an ark on the flood waters. A
house can endure and remain in good condition even
if its occupants are evil or have long since abandoned
it. The New Testament, therefore, corrects this misconception when it emphasizes in the first letter of
Peter (2, 5) that the members of the Church are themselves the living stones to be built into a spiritual
house. We cannot view the visible Church by looking
beyond the people of whom she is built, and whose
personal decision must bring her into being. Although
the Church has been built once and for all by Jesus
Christ, the New Testament reminds us that we must
build one another up.

Thus we cannot, on the one hand, concede that the
individual people in the Church are in need of reform
and, on the other hand, reject as unnecessary a renewal
and reform of the Church, as though the Church were
a kind of ideal institution that should not be disturbed
when the people of the Church become evil and need
to be called to conversion.

A similar danger of misunderstanding lies in the idea
of the Church, quite true in itself, as the sign of the
Lord's presence in human history. The Church really is
a *sacramentum salutis,* a token and pledge to man of
God's saving grace. That is precisely why she is visible.
However, we must not conclude from this that the
Church, as a sign for humanity, is something different
and set apart from the humanity to whom she pro-

claims salvation. No. She becomes real as a sign from God through the people living in her.

Therefore, the visible aspect of the Church, so strongly emphasized by our faith, must mean at least the humanity of the Church. She is present in men and is made up of men, who in baptism have become members of the Church, who are redeemed from original sin itself, but who are not freed of its consequences, and are therefore quite subject to criticism. Where could we possibly find an institution, no matter how perfectly designed by its founder, which in human hands would not be a distortion of what was originally intended? It is part of the mystery of the Church — and this must be taken seriously by her critics — that to a great extent she demonstrates her divine character by continuing to live and to be effective despite all that might provoke criticism of her.

Criticism of the Church is therefore a *real possibility;* in fact it is a duty. That the official spokesmen of the Church often enough react defensively to criticism is not so remarkable when we consider that most of the criticism is directed against those spokesmen, when actually it fits equally well the great mass of Church members — and the critics themselves. Fundamentally, the Church herself has endorsed men's right and duty to criticize her in her constant efforts toward reform. Vatican Council II was convened, in the final analysis, for the sake of renewal in the Church and to stress the commission originally given her by Jesus Christ. There is no other course open if the Church is to profess to be the visible and human institution of Christ. This "institution" differs from an institution that is of a technical construction because her appeal is to human decision and her tasks are to be realized by human efforts. These efforts must be constantly reexamined by those to whom they apply. They must also be scrutinized by those others, who are not always objective in their judgment but are just as subjective in their way as those criticized.

Thus, criticism of the Church is not only possible; it has an *important function*. It is another form of reminder and incentive to strive for that ideal which even in the Church is never fully attained, but must be striven for. Criticism can and should thrust the Church directly into that eschatological attitude in which she looks toward her final form as the kingdom of God. The Church must not only live in hope in the sense that she awaits fulfillment and consummation as a gift that will someday come to her. In this sense eschatological hope could actually become a form of escape from the reality that the critics are attacking. The Church's hope should also be a hope that reaches out and seeks to achieve what is not yet achieved; if she has achieved something, she should continue to challenge the achievement. Precisely when it is most disquieting, criticism guards the Church against the danger of sitting smugly satisfied and comfortable in her hope. Genuine constructive criticism points out weaknesses in order to stir up strength to overcome them. To reach a goal we must not only keep it in view, so that we will be attracted to it; we must also see the inadequacy of our achievements, so that we will be startled and perhaps even shocked into action.

Criticism that points out defects in view of positive goals is constructive criticism, because it does not deny the hidden but vital elements in what is criticized; instead, it awakens them. This kind of criticism, by pointing to the negative elements, marks the beginning of their removal and thus the discovery of the positive ones. Perhaps critics could test the integrity of their purpose by asking themselves whether they are really concerned with urging the Church they criticize onto the road toward the kingdom of God, whether they see the Church as already on the way, and in their criticism are roadblocks to the Church's progress. Is their criticism, instead, motivated more by a secret delight in failure, an unacknowledged feeling that the Church can do no better, or a general attitude of hopelessness?

There cannot be much objection to a crticism, including a criticism of the Church, that is made *publicly*. Even within the Church there is certainly a kind of criticism that is in line with Christ's norms for fraternal correction. The Lord spoke of reprimand "between the two of you alone", or in the presence of one or two witnesses (Matt. 18, 15f.), in cases when some mistake, though detrimental to the Church, originated from the wrong conduct of an individual. In such cases it is also necessary to criticize the individual and *his* misdeed or wrong attitude. To make that kind of criticism public, however, would in the case of the Church be as objectionable as in any other area of human relations.

There is, however, a kind of criticism of the Church that can be legitimately made public, for the Church is essentially a public human community. To make religion only a private matter, to locate faith only in individual encounter with God — or to regard the Church as seemingly the sum of individuals equally disposed to faith — is certainly counter to what Christian faith, in any case Catholic faith, believes from the New Testament about the Church as the institution of Christ. The Church is not merely communal, faithful practice. The Church is so very much a public manifestation of Christ in human society that this publicly oriented Church must be regarded as the

Church to whom God primarily addresses himself, communicating his Word and salvation to individuals by incorporating them as her members. It is therefore unavoidable that the Church be the subject of public discussion and argument. If she were not, we might fear that she had become unfaithful to her essential task. If the Church experiences public criticism, it is likely that she will defend herself against rash, biased judgments and propagandistic distortions. However, such public criticism also permits her to see that she is still faithful to her essential task of publicly witnessing to what she possesses. Otherwise public criticism would of course have no visible point of articulation.

Precisely because visibility and publicity are not merely incidental features to be tolerated, but are an important aspect of the Church, there is no resorting to an alibi that distinguishes between "Church" and "Catholicism" whenever criticism is encountered. The Church cannot shift critical blame over onto a Catholicism that is something other than the Church herself; nor can critics who are accused of irreverence or lack of restraint take refuge in the alibi that they were referring to Catholicism but not to the Church.

In certain situations it is meaningful to make a distinction between Catholicism and the Church. The Church is not involved with equal depth and intensity in all areas of the lives of her faithful. Perhaps there are areas still so remotely related to the Church that, even though they are included in the concept of Catholicism, they are not so closely involved with the Church that they could be called ecclesiastical. Here a distinction between Church and Catholicism makes some sense. However, it still does not provide much opportunity for excuse in the face of criticism, for criticism is involved with the concrete areas of human life. However, since the Church is necessarily what people mean by Catholicism, then Catholicism is the Church in its effect in the human areas of existence. Consequently, if Catholicism is subjected to criticism, the Church must take this criticism upon herself; likewise anyone criticizing Catholicism must realize he is also criticizing the Church.

Thus, the critic of the Church cannot by evasion treat Catholicism this way — trying to exclude from criticism only the "sacred elements" of the Church, so as to criticize Catholicism all the more freely. The basic admission we must make about the possibility of criticism is an admission about criticism of the *Church,* for it is to the pilgrim Church that Christ has given a visible and human character.

THE DIFFICULTY IN CRITICIZING THE CHURCH

In saying "yes" to criticism of the Church we must, however, enter a qualification at the very outset. It should be emphasized of course that this qualification cannot turn the "yes" to a "no". It is much more a question of the difficulties inherent in criticism of the Church. Pointing these out will serve to make criticism of the Church more helpful, for only if there is an awareness of the difficulties involved can criticism be meaningful. These difficulties primarily arise from factors that the Church has in common with other living realities, having social and historical dimensions, but permeated by the supernatural mystery of the *holy* Church.

The Life of the Church as a Community

With regard to the Church as a living *community,*

to be realized by persons and imbued with the grace of God, there are three factors that are especially relevant to the problem of criticism.

First, the Church as a living community is ambivalent in her relationship to the world. In St. John's Gospel, we are told that Jesus, the high priest, says in his prayer for his disciples that they are "not of the world", but that he has "sent them into the world". He says these things while comparing his disciples' situation with that of his own: "even as I am not of the world", and "as thou hast sent me into the world". Ever since, the Church has been called "ecclesia". This is not of course a purely linguistic matter; yet there is this literal meaning: she has been "called out" of the world and is therefore different from, if not separate from, the world. She must not be of the world. And yet she has always known that she was sent into the world, is planted in the world and is even, so to speak, a piece of the world, but a piece in which "world" is transformed into that unique reality permeated by the saving presence of Christ.

Because of her situation in the world, the Church is seen as something akin to men, something tangible, and thus open to critical discussion. Because they find themselves in the same world as the Church, her critics believe they know the criteria by which the Church should be judged. In part they are right, of course, but only in part. However near the Church is to the world, she is nevertheless so very different from the world that she cannot be judged and criticized from the outside. One must himself live the life of the Church if he is to accurately know her and the faith prescribed for her. Only then will he be able to judge whether and to what extent she is fulfilling her vocation or reprehensibly falling below it. This being-in-the-

Church is not fulfilled by mere membership in the visible Church. Very many members of the visible Church do not live her life as truly as some others who are not part of the visible and sacramental Church in the full sense, but who nevertheless discern and live the inward life and who share in the concerns, and understand the salvific meaning, of the Church. Keeping this in mind, we can and must say: valid judgment and criticism of the Church can come only from one who not only observes the living Church from the outside, but also experiences her inner life. For that very reason a statement such as the following is questionable: *"Sentire cum Ecclesia* (to think with the Church) may require us to break with existing Catholicism." Incidentally, Ignatius of Loyola, from whose *Spiritual Exercises* the phrase, *Sentire cum Ecclesia,* is taken, does not call his admonitions, *Rules for Right Thinking with the Church,* but rather *Rules for Right Thinking in the Church*.

There is a second factor, closely connected with the first one, that makes criticism of the Church as a living community a difficult matter. The Church cannot avert the danger of secularization by simply refusing to deal with the immoral of this world, for in that case, in the words of Saint Paul, "you would have to leave the world" (1 Cor. 5, 9f.). Because she is a temporal reality rooted in the world just as Christ himself, as a true man having taken on the form of a servant, was rooted in the world, the Church must *bear within her very much of the form of the world*. And yet she must not do this to the extent that she ceases to be Church in distinction to the "world" (understood in the Johannine sense).

This, however, opens up a large area of questions and decisions involving human judgment, such as

whether and to what extent the Church's temporal
existence should be given concrete form; whether it is
more meaningful to adopt this or that method of temporal action and attitude in the Church's mode of
existence in the world; whether it would be better to
use this or that means of influencing environment.
Questions like these have no single clear answer. What
is involved is the decision of human intelligence guided
by faith. No detailed proof is needed to show that there
is ample room here for legitimate criticism of the
Church. Criticism must not, however, judge too hastily
the institutional suitability of a specific ecclesiastical
action, even though this can occasionally be a criterion
in judging whether the action was intelligent and in
keeping with the goal of the Church. This is much
easier to do, of course, *after* the situation in which the
decision had to be made. In this area such criticism
should always leave open the possibility that others
might have a different criterion for the same problem.

There is a third factor that makes criticism of the
ecclesiastical community difficult. As a salvific community called forth from the world by the Lord, the
Church looks like a small flock amid the enormous
mass of people outside her. She therefore possesses
somehow an elite character and must, consequently,
make demands on herself, i.e., on her members, that
are not made on most men. Therefore, in judging what
it sees and experiences of the Church, criticism simply
cannot help using the sort of criterion applicable to
any elite group of individuals who ought to be above
average.

And yet the Church is at the same time a kind of
embodiment of the universal salvific will of God, "who
wishes all men to be saved" (1 Tim. 2, 4). Thus the
Church is a reality situated between an elect who actu-

ally experiences her (an election that can be reserved
only to the few) and the mass of people, practically
synonymous with what is called the world. The Church
must, therefore, continually move dynamically forward,
summoning those entrusted to her to surpass their
present achievement. The shepherds of the Church,
however, will always have to steer a course that will
enable those members who are not called to heroism
to live within her and, in her, to penitently overcome
the sins of weakness and apathy — in short, to be able
to be at home within her, even as sinners. This makes a
fair criticism of the Church very difficult. It is to supply
the kind of criticism that will seriously face the fact of
sin and scandal in the Church, even though these things
should not be. Certainly the Church must constantly
do penance for sin and for complacency toward the
world, and turn from these. However, criticism should
see as incredible and indefensible, not only the fact of
sin and compromise but also the slowness and dubious-
ness of many decisions. To remain realistic in this
matter is really not easy, since of course it is impossible
to set up a program of peaceful coexistence between
Christian faith and atheism.

So much for the difficulty of criticizing the Church
in terms of a living community. Criticism of the Church
becomes no less difficult when we consider her as a
continuation in history.

Historicity of the Church

Criticism also has its rights and limitations with regard to the Church as an historical reality. Christ
founded his Church and promised to preserve her from
destruction. This institution is, however, an historical

fact in the twofold sense that it took place in history
and works through history. The Church was established
in history and is thus derived from historical forces.
These forces can be judged by the original norm. However, they are also subject to other criteria, for history
is a march through time, determined by free human
decisions and in turn influencing these decisions.

Criticism of the Church has a great task here. It
makes us aware that something is not necessarily shown
to be as Christ wanted it simply because it has been
carried along throughout a long history. Criticism repeatedly poses the crucial question of whether a feature
in the life of the Church is retained because Christ
himself wanted it, or because the circumstances that
gave rise to it persist, or perhaps because we are too
weak or too lazy to surrender or alter what is outdated,
yielding to more contemporary forms and arrangements.
If it is historical in its approach, such criticism should
also admit the difficulties besetting it — whether it is
concerned with something past or something present.
Such criticism necessarily looks through *contemporary*
eyes at a segment of ecclesiastical life no longer present
today. This difficulty of the "no-longer-present" feature
of historical reality as seen by the critic holds true, it
seems to me, not only when he seeks to judge the past.
The observer of history cannot be deprived of the right
to go beyond a kind of Rankian objectivism which
would insist that the historian portray only what has
happened. No, we have learned to differentiate between
history and narrative. Historical observation means
more than inventories of facts; it means adopting a
position and evaluating history for the present and the
future. Such an evaluation of history is impossible
without some kind of express judgment of the past.
Yet this judgment is difficult because the events of the

past can be seen only in a very fragmentary way, without their living connections, without the totality and complexity of the life of the age when they happened. This difficulty is also pertinent to criticism in the present, criticism of the Church here and now. Whatever exists and is operative today was extensively determined by history. Thus in order to criticize fairly, objectively and realistically, we must consider history in our judgments. Therefore, the difficulty we encounter in trying to fairly and realistically criticize the historical past is also inherent in the criticism of the present.

This is all the more true of the Church as a subject of criticism, a Church that did not simply take place in the past like the eruption of Vesuvius in Pompeii in 79 A.D., but is a community of persons making their way together through human history and yet reflecting a wide variety of individual human decisions and interrelations. If it is true, however, that we cannot objectively judge a spiritually vital community of individuals, unless we live the life of that community in a way proper to it and participate positively in the decisions forming that life, then criticism has reached a serious limitation. It is subject to a requirement that it cannot completely satisfy. For it is of course a truth of our faith that the Church in which we live today is the same Church which has come through history from the founding hand of Christ, and that therefore her life is today essentially like that of the earlier centuries. Viewed in this way, we are therefore really in the Church that we are criticizing. It is just as true, however, that the historicity of this Church means that she also differed during those earlier centuries from the Churches of today. This makes criticism of the Church difficult not only when we moderns critically judge or even condemn, for example, the medieval crusades or the Church's imperial ties. It is almost equally true of a judgment as to whether and to what extent German Catholicism capitulated to Hitler two decades ago.

It should be emphasized once again: pointing out these difficulties does not mean that we cannot and should not try to present things just as they were, even though they may be painful, reprehensible and all too human. Nor does it mean that we may not form a judgment, a criticism, in order to determine what ought to have happened. The caution derived from considering these difficulties, however, will help criticism fulfill its proper role and, in any case, it should prevent critics from assuming that only certain motivating factors lay behind the attitudes of bygone times, while they overlook a whole host of other factors or mitigating circumstances.

Criticism and the Holiness of the Church

Both in content and in tone, therefore, criticism must indicate that the things under attack are not simply evils coexisting parallel to much that is good, but that these same things criticized as evils also contain good. This good must be acknowledged, even though it is a defective good. What is required then is the conscientiousness previously mentioned: both sides of the question must be considered; the critic must also show that consideration for the weak so strongly emphasized by Saint Paul, for to the weak an objectively justified attitude might become a scandal. The critic must also be ready to admit that his own critical competence has limitations and needs to be supplemented. Furthermore, he should be aware of reasons for restraint and discretion. The above-mentioned modification of a completely honest and well-intended admission to criticism of the Church, and especially the appeal above to conscience, are further confirmed if we believe in the mystery that the Church is, even in her concrete form as Catholicism and in her manifest incompleteness. This mystery has for ages been traditionally reflected in the Church's attribute of "holiness". This attribute would naturally provoke challenge if it implied that the Church contained within her only individuals whose personal lives were holy. The tension here, however, is precisely because she is a holy Church by reason of her mysterious sharing in Christ's divine manhood, and yet at the same time she is actualized in such unholy men.

To profess that they are the holy Church is a humiliating duty for her sincere members. However, it is their duty, because holiness is imparted to the Church by the active presence of the Lord within her; it is only to a slight extent due to the moral sanctity of her people. This faith in the Church's holiness now confirms both factors in a way that appeals to conscience: restraint and caution in criticism are no longer determined only by the difficulties that criticism must reckon with, but also by a God-given holiness, and with it an inviolable quality peculiar to holy things. At the same time, however, considerations of human fulfillment in the Church become more critical, because the objective holiness present in the incarnate mystery of the Church makes increased demands on the efforts and decisions of her members.

There was also the possibility of criticism in the case of Jesus Christ, the God-Man, for he took on the form of a servant and thus subjected himself to human judgments. They fell to his lot in abundance. Yet the New Testament shows that faith removes the Lord from human criticism, because this faith gives adoration to

the God present within him, whose holiness and inviolability are also shared by the human figure of Jesus,
that belongs to the person of the divine Logos. Not to
take the humanity of Jesus Christ sufficiently seriously
has on occasion endangered Christian piety. Thus the
criticism leveled at the man Jesus during his earthly
life was possible, but it was unjustified because the
human conduct of Jesus corresponded in every respect
to God's presence within him.

The Church has a genuine share in the divine incarnation and thus in the holiness of Jesus Christ, but only
a share. In her the human element is truly sanctified
by the work of God. However, it is unfortunately not
true that human behavior within the Church always
corresponds to the presence of God. Thus criticism of
the Church's holiness is not only possible, as was criticism of Christ, but it is also justified to a great extent.
Nevertheless, she is the mysterious body of the Lord.
This means not only that there is a vitality of spirit
present in her, such as might objectively permeate human societies in varying degrees, but also that the life
of God is in her. Due to this divine life, she is able
to survive not only hostile forces from without and the
much more threatening wretchedness from within; she
also possesses a holiness and an inviolability that must
be taken seriously also by her critics. A disrespectful
criticism has no cause to wonder why it is immediately
rejected by those who are convinced of and imbued
by the charismatic holiness of the Church. By the same
token, they of course run the risk of rejecting criticism
even where it is necessary and justified.

Finally, we must not forget how difficult it is for
people to overcome the tension that comes from having
to defend a holy Church externally and to achieve her
holiness inwardly, while yet experiencing in themselves

how unholy they may cause the holy Church to appear in the eyes of the world. It will surely be necessary again and again for prophetic storms to sweep in against the human laziness, presumption, unkindness, rigid environmental bonds, and whatever else is wrong in the Church. Criticism of the Church will have to determine whether its attack is the kind of prophecy called forth on behalf of the holy God in the Church sanctified by him, or whether it is really only human impatience or even intolerance, a criticism that no longer reflects the belief: "The foolish things of the world has God chosen to put to shame the 'wise.'"

STUDY-CLUB QUESTIONS

1. Is the Church open to criticism? Is the right to criticize unlimited?
2. What precisely do we mean by the visible Church? How can this "visibility" be misinterpreted?
3. What function does criticism perform? Is all criticism constructive? What is the criterion?
4. In considering the Church as an historical reality, what crucial question does criticism pose?
5. What are the difficulties of judging the Church historically?
6. What does historical observation entail?
7. Why should we be cautious in expressing a critical attitude?
8. Did Christ submit himself to human judgments? How?
9. In what ways can the Church be said to be holy?
10. What does the Church's holiness imply in regard to criticism?